Praise for *Julian of Norwich: The Showings*

"As a major fan and promoter of Julian of Norwich, whom I call 'my favorite mystic,' it is genuinely exciting to find such a faithful but freeing translation of Julian's long lost *Showings*. Now they are no longer lost—for anyone!"

—FR. RICHARD ROHR, O.F.M.,
CENTER FOR ACTION AND CONTEMPLATION

"Julian of Norwich deserves as wide a readership as possible today for her wise, deep, and spirited telling of the Christ story along with the Motherhood of God. Her teachings are sorely needed to balance out the pessimism and patriarchal overload we find in today's culture and religion. Mirabai's translation is fresh and readable, helping to render Julian very alive and edgy still after all these years. We should all be thankful for this gift from Julian and Mirabai."

—MATTHEW FOX, AUTHOR OF *ORIGINAL BLESSING*,
A SPIRITUALITY NAMED COMPASSION, AND
*HILDEGARD OF BINGEN, A SAINT FOR OUR TIMES:
UNLEASHING HER POWER IN THE 21ST CENTURY*

"Julian of Norwich's *Showings* shines with luminous mystical wisdom—and Mirabai Starr's lovely and engaging translation of this medieval masterpiece makes it more accessible than ever."

—CARL MCCOLMAN, AUTHOR OF *THE BIG BOOK OF CHRISTIAN MYSTICISM* AND *ANSWERING THE CONTEMPLATIVE CALL*

JULIAN OF NORWICH
The Showings

Uncovering the Face of the Feminine in
Revelations of Divine Love

MIRABAI STARR

Foreword by Richard Rohr

Cover design by Kathryn Sky-Peck
Cover art by Erin Currier © Erin Currier Fine Art
Interior by Jane Hagaman

Hampton Roads Publishing Company, Inc.
Charlottesville, VA 22906
Distributed by Red Wheel/Weiser, LLC
www.redwheelweiser.com

Sign up for our newsletter and special offers by going to
www.redwheelweiser.com/newsletter.

ISBN 978-1-64297-036-4

Library of Congress Cataloging-in-Publication Data

Printed in the United States of America
IBI

10 9 8 7 6 5 4 3 2 1

I saw three ways to look at the Motherhood of God. The first is that she created our human nature. The second is that she took our human nature upon herself, which is where the motherhood of grace begins. And the third is motherhood in action, in which she spreads herself throughout all that is, penetrating everything with grace, extending to the fullest length and breadth, height and depth. All One Love.

—JULIAN OF NORWICH

Contents

PART I: REVELATION OF LOVE

PART II: EVERY KIND OF THING SHALL BE WELL

PART III: YOU WILL NOT BE OVERCOME

Foreword

This beautiful word "mother" is so sweet and kind in itself
that it cannot be attributed to anyone but God.
—Julian of Norwich

In this citation from *Julian of Norwich: The Showings,* Lady Julian offers us an amazing and foundational statement. She is not saying that the most beloved attributes of motherhood can analogously be applied to God, although I am sure she would agree they could. She is saying much more—that the very word *mother* is so definitive and "beautiful" in most peoples' experience (not everybody's, I must add) that it evokes, at its best, what we mean by God— which is "sweetness" and "kindness." Except for their mystics, this is *not* what most of the world's religions have taught or believed up to now. Among these, Julian of Norwich stands as pivotal.

The concept and human experience of mother is so primal, so big, deep, universal, and wide that to apply it only to our own mothers is way too small a container. It can only be applied to God. Do any of us realize how revolutionary this is? Mother is, for Julian, the best descriptor for God Herself! I use this to illustrate the courageous, original, and yet fully orthodox character of Julian's teaching—especially in the hands of a likeminded translator like Mirabai Starr.

Julian helps me finally understand one major aspect of my own Catholic culture: why in heaven's name, for 1,500 years, did both the Eastern and Western churches attribute almost everything beautiful and beloved, every shrine, hill, cathedral, protection, blessing, statue, and most classic art in the Middle East and Europe, not usually to Jesus, or even to God, but to some iteration of Mother Mary? I have always thought it was scripturally weak but psychologically brilliant. Many people in Julian's time did not read much scripture—in fact most could not read at all. They interpreted at the level of archetype and symbol. The "word" or logos was quite good, but a feminine image for God, a transformative symbol like Sophia, was even better.

However, this seemed to later sola scriptura (by scripture alone) traditions like a huge aberration, a major misplacement of attention, or even an outright heresy. Yet, that is how much the soul needed a Mother Savior and a God Nurturer! In a profoundly patriarchal, hierarchical, judgmental, exclusionary, imperial, and warlike period of history and Christianity, I believe it was probably necessary and salutary. I fully agree with Carl Jung who believed that the soul creates the images it needs for its own wholeness and healing. If it doesn't, we have some form of toxic religion, in which God is a tyrant and eternal punisher. This is not the God of Julian's belief.

I would go so far to say that the reason most religions in the last millennia overdid the notion of God as male is precisely to overcompensate for what was almost too obvious: God is, in essence, like a good mother—so compassionate that there was no need to compete with a Father God—as we see in Julian's always balanced teachings. Mother Mary is always holding, presenting, protecting, and pushing forward her male son—often with his little penis in full view: Almighty God and Vulnerable God as one.

I begin with this observation because it so well illustrates the radical freedom and optimism, no doubt entirely experiential, and intuitive, of this 14th-century English laywoman. I sincerely doubt if she could have thought, much less written such things as this if she had been male, ordained, powerful, scholastically educated, or even a member of an established order of nuns. She reveals this in her many referrals to herself as obedient, submissive, "even Christian," and also in withholding her opinion if "Holy Church" teaches differently. Julian knew how to play the clerical field, after first—and usually convincingly—making her own point. She was not a rebel, just a very good player.

Ever since I first discovered Julian thirty years ago and especially after I stayed in her hermitage in Norwich shortly afterward, I have always considered her to be my favorite mystic—with Thérèse of Lisieux, John of the Cross, Bonaventure, Teresa of Ávila, and Francis of Assisi all in the running. Now, with this so readable and truly inspired translation by my dear friend Mirabai, I have found my favorite translation of my favorite mystic. Could it be because Mirabai is also a laywoman, a mother and daughter herself (I know her dear mother and have stayed in her munchkin house), not scholastically educated (thank God), not powerful, but a good Jewish woman just like Mary?

Mirabai is her own real kind of mystic, who nurtures and enlightens all she meets at her interspirituality conferences and at delicious lunches on her flower-filled patio. She grew up a bit of a hippie and a free spirit around the grounds of the famous Lama Foundation north of Taos. If you read Mirabai's memoir,

Caravan of No Despair, you learn that one of her own beloved daughters died tragically, very young, in an auto accident. This whole and delightful woman is herself daughter, mother, Pietà, spiritual teacher, translator par excellence, and wife to another loving mystic, Jeff Little (Ganga Das). Every group she is with thinks she is one of them, she moves so easily in their company and with their vocabularies of holiness.

I am so honored to write these few words to lead you toward two of my favorite women. Now allow Mirabai to show you Julian's "Showings"—and you will see beauty twice.

—RICHARD ROHR, AUTHOR OF *FALLING UPWARD*

Acknowledgments

With profound gratitude to the guides who opened the way for me to encounter such an extraordinary being as Julian of Norwich: Amy Frykholm, Dr. Fred Roden, Carl McColman, and, most especially, Frs. William Hart McNichols and Richard Rohr, whose profound love for Julian makes me love her even more. To Matthew Fox, who shows how Julian's revelations of divine love are precise medicine for these times. To Greg Brandenburgh for reaching out and giving me wings. To my Jewish mother, Susanna, who cries when Julian promises us that Christ-the-Mother promised her that "All will be well." And to the most supportive and insightful person I know, my husband, Ganga Das. Finally, to Lady Julian, who so companionably sat beside me as I endeavored to transmit the living waters of her wisdom.

Introduction

All will be well and all will be well
and every kind of thing shall be well.

The Face of the Holy One

You have been to the threshold of death and felt the breath of eternity on your eyelids. You don't need the appointed intermediaries to tell you about the Holy One: you have had a direct encounter, and it has changed you. When they speak about "God's will" and tell you exactly how to interpret it, you stifle a chuckle and try to look pious. You have gone riding wild horses with the Holy One along a rocky seashore under the full moon. They warn you about impure thoughts, but the God you love is an unconditionally loving mother who squeezes your cheeks, looks into your eyes, and tells you that you are the most adorable creature she ever created.

Ever since that troublemaker Eve handed that gullible Adam the fruit of the Tree of the Knowledge of Good and Evil, they say, human beings have been continuously messing up and suffering the consequences. But in the depths of your darkest despair your Beloved calls to you: "Look," he says, and opens the fathomless beautiful wound of his heart so that you can peer inside. All creation is nestled there, bathed in beauty. "Do you see any sin here?" he asks. "Do you detect a shred of retribution?" You do not. All you perceive, from horizon to endless horizon, is love. As far as your eye can see there stretches a line of joyous children being welcomed home.

The God you have met does not want your self-recrimination. You have already paid the price for your stumbling. You have endured the sorrow and weariness ignorance brings. Your God would never punish you for being a human being: this life itself is your penance, she reminds you. But it is also more than that: it is a crucible for transformation. Each trial, every loss, is an opportunity for you to meet suffering with love and make of it an offering, a prayer. The minute you lift your pain like a candle the darkness vanishes, and mercy comes rushing in to heal you.

The Showings

She was a thirty-year-old medieval Englishwoman having a near-death experience. She almost didn't make it through the night. As she felt her soul begin to slip away, she had a vision of Christ, followed by fifteen more over the course of the next few hours, which she spent the next two decades unpacking, winnowing, and interpreting for the sake of all spiritual seekers everywhere. This is about all we know of the woman we call Julian of Norwich. And that may not even have been her real name. The attribution comes down to us only by virtue of the enclosure she dwelled inside of, never leaving, cobbled to the north wall of the Church of St. Julian in the town of Norwich, England.

By the time Julian survived her life-threatening illness, she had already witnessed multiple rounds of the black death, which had wiped out a huge swath of the population. She was familiar with suffering. She refers a couple of times to having lost the will to live in the wake of the hardships and sorrows of this world. I imagine that at her age she must have been married and borne children, but the only relative she speaks of is her mother, who never left her side as she lay dying. I can't help but wonder if she had lost the rest of her family to the plague, watching husband and babies succumb to the ravaging disease, helpless to save them. How could her own death be anything but a welcome reprieve from a life of such tragedy?

She also asked for it. When Julian was young, she confesses, in the throes of spiritual idealism, she prayed for three "graces": one, to bear witness to the passion of Christ; two, to endure an illness serious enough to carry her to the brink of death but not beyond; and three, to experience the triple-wound of contrition, compassion, and longing for God. Her prayer was answered. She became so ill that the priest was called to administer last rites. She had a vision of Jesus dying on the cross before her eyes, his copiously flowing blood enough to have splashed up the walls of her room. And the teachings that Christ gave to her filled her heart with humility, empathy for all suffering beings, and a burning yearning for union with God, which she refers to as "oneing."

As soon as she was well enough to sit up, she began to record every detail of the sixteen showings revealed to her as she hovered on the threshold of death. This account is known in the literature as the "Short Text." Twenty years later, having ensconced herself in a small cell where she alternately dedicated herself to solitary prayer and cheerful spiritual direction through the single window that faced the street, Julian began to fill out her notes with reflections on the meaning of her visions, which comprise the "Long Text" (the version you find translated here).

At the end of her writings, Julian asks what the Holy One meant by all this. "Would you like to know?" comes the response. "Know it well: love was his meaning. Who revealed this to you? Love. What did he reveal to you? Love. Why did he reveal it to you? For love. Stay with this and you will know more of the same. You will never know anything but love, without end."

No Such Thing

Julian of Norwich is known for her radically optimistic theology. Nowhere is this better illumined than in her reflections on sin. When Julian asked God to teach her about this troubling issue, he opened his Divine Being, and all she could see there was love. Every lesser truth dissolved in that boundless ocean. She tried with all her might to line up what she had learned from the Church and what her Beloved directly revealed to her.

"But the truth is," Julian confesses, "I did not see any sin. I believe that sin has no substance, not a particle of being, and cannot be detected at all except by the pain it causes. It is only the pain that has substance, for a while, and it serves to purify us, and make us know ourselves and ask for mercy."

Julian informs us that the suffering we cause ourselves through our acts of greed and unconsciousness is the only punishment we endure. God, who is All-Love, is "incapable of wrath." And so it is a complete waste of time, Julian realized, to wallow in guilt. The truly humble thing to do when we have stumbled is to hoist ourselves to our feet as swiftly as we can and rush into the arms of God where we will remember who we really are.

For Julian, sin has no substance because it is the *absence* of all that is good and kind, loving and caring—all that is of God. Sin is nothing but separation from our divine source. And separation from the Holy One is nothing but illusion. We are always and forever "oned" in love with our Beloved. Therefore, sin is not real; only love is real. Julian did not require a Divinity degree to arrive at this conclusion. She simply needed to travel to the boundary-land of death where she was enfolded in the loving embrace of the Holy One, who assured her that he had loved her since before he made her and would love her till the end of time. And it is with this great love, he revealed, that he loves all beings. Our only task is to remember this and rejoice.

In the end, Julian says, it will all be clear. "Then none of us will be moved in any way to say, *Lord, if only things had been different, all would have been well,*" she writes. "Instead, we shall all proclaim in one voice, *Beloved One, may you be blessed, because it is so: all* is *well.*"

God-the-Mother

The fact that Julian "saw no wrath in God" does not tempt her to engage in harmful behaviors with impunity. On the contrary, the freedom she finds in God's unconditional love makes her strive even more to be worthy of his mercy and grace. Yet she does not waste energy on regret. She suggests that we, too, would be wise to shift our attention away from our own small selves and our petty human foibles and get on with the holy task of loving God with all our hearts and all our minds and all our strength. Julian even perceives the crucifixion of Christ through the lens of love, revealing not a mask of anguish but a "sweet and friendly countenance" which radiates courtesy and affection. It is in this spirit that she names God "The Mother."

"This beautiful word 'mother' is so sweet and kind in itself that it cannot be attributed to anyone but God," Julian declares.

"Only he who is our true Mother and source of all life may rightfully be called by this name. Nature, love, wisdom, and knowledge are all attributes of the Mother, which is God."

Who else but a mother would pour herself out and break herself open for her children? Who but a mother would nurture life inside her own body and maintain a garden where we can take refuge and grow strong? Julian informs us that she "saw three ways to look at the Motherhood of God. The first," she says, "is that she created our human nature. The second is that she took our human nature upon herself, which is where the motherhood of grace begins. And the third is motherhood in action, in which she spreads herself throughout all that is, penetrating everything with grace, extending to the fullest length and breadth, height and depth. All One Love."

God-the-Mother, according to Julian's view, is identical with the Second Person of the Holy Trinity: Christ. "God chose to become our Mother in all ways," Julian writes, "humbly and tenderly cultivating the ground of his work in the womb of a maiden. Our transcendent God, the glorious wisdom of the universe, emptied himself into this earthy place and made himself entirely available through our own poor flesh. In this form he himself offered the unconditional service and duties of motherhood. Being nearest to our own nature, the mother's serving is most immediate. Being unconditionally loving, the mother's service is most willing. And being the truest thing there is, the mother's service is most certain. Only God could ever perform such duty."

This breathes a little balance into the conventional doctrines, doesn't it? Through the unshakable certainty she has regarding the veracity of her visions, Julian unapologetically introduces God-the-Father, the exalted source of all Power; God-the-Mother (who is also the God-the-Son), the indwelling source of all Wisdom; and God-the-Holy-Spirit, the ever-present source of all

Goodness, who transcends gender and permeates all things: All One Love.

A Light in the Darkness

What does Julian of Norwich, a fourteenth-century Catholic anchoress, who spent the majority of her adult life cloistered in a small stone cell attached to a church, have to teach us here and now? She reveals the feminine face of the Divine in all its radiance and reminds us to seek God there. She teaches us that God's love has nothing to do with rules and retribution and everything to do with mercy and compassion. She shows us that our failings and transgressions are simply an opportunity to learn and grow, and should be honored as such, but not dwelled upon. She translates the sorrows of this life as tastes of Christ's passion and assures us that all passing pain will be transmuted into endless joy.

Most of all, Julian of Norwich promises that, in spite of appearances to the contrary, all is well. Not just that creation was beautifully made to begin with, and that it will all work out in the end, but that everything is all right at every moment, if we could only look through the eyes of love. Such a perspective is difficult to sustain, Julian would be the first to admit. In rare moments of unitive consciousness—watching the sun rise, maybe, or giving birth, or singing to God in community—we may have fleeting glimpses of the cosmic design and see that it is good. But then the veil drops again and we forget. We succumb to the illusion that we are worthless wretches and life a cruel conspiracy.

Thankfully, we have guides to light the path back home. Mystics of every age and all religious traditions have held aloft beacons of ecstatic poetry and elegant prose. From Francis of Assisi to Teresa of Avila, from Rumi to Rabia, from Walt Whitman to Lucille Clifton, reminders of the wild beauty and never-ending love of the Divine abound. Julian of Norwich's message is as relevant now as it was in the Middle Ages: God loves us completely, exactly as we are.

"Then he showed me a small thing, the size of a hazelnut, nestled in the palm of my hand," Julian writes. "It was round as a ball. I looked at it with the eyes of my understanding and thought, *What can this be?* And the answer came to me: *It is all that is created.* I was amazed that it could continue to exist. It seemed to me to be so little that it was on the verge of dissolving into nothingness. And then these words entered my understanding: *It lasts, and will last forever, because God loves it. Everything that is has its being through the love of God.*"

A Note on the Translation

Julian of Norwich offers us some delicious morsels of language in her original text that did not make it to your table. It does not work to transform a Middle English text into an accessible teaching for contemporary sensibilities with all of the original arcane phraseology sprinkled in. It interrupts the flow. But I can't resist sharing a few tantalizing tastes of what you're missing here.

Julian refers to God as "homely." This doesn't mean funny-looking or plain. Homely refers to the essential "friendliness" of the Divine. Julian's God is not some inaccessible father figure who rules from on high; he is her intimate companion and most familiar loved one.

In addition to such charming yet awkward words, Julian uses certain terms that fit for her time but which I feel could alienate my contemporaries—particularly those among us who are not Christians yet are on a serious path of spiritual awakening and seek wisdom teachings in multiple traditions. Therefore, I changed the evocative term "my even Christians" to "my fellow spiritual seekers" and "those who will be saved" as "all beings." I sometimes call "our faith" and "the Church" "our spiritual community," though I did retain "Holy Church" when it directly referred to Julian's struggle to line up the radically transformational aspects of her visions with the "ordinary teachings" (as she called them) of the only religion she knew: the Roman Catholicism of the Middle Ages.

While Julian often calls God her Beloved, she also refers to him as Lord on many occasions. In the spirit of inclusivity—which I see as specially aligned with Julian's insights—Beloved is the default name in my translation. After all, this is a mystic who freely says that God is also our Mother, gently and lovingly defying the patriarchy at almost every turn. I sometimes call heaven "the world-to-come." The devil is "the spirit of evil" and the "Fiend" is "the Adversary."

There were other terms I could not bring myself to alter, such as "well and woe." Again and again, Julian (like the Buddha) acknowledges that this life is a continuous flow of suffering and joy, and that everything changes. She points us in the direction of the more real thing underlying the passing phenomena of the relative world. But "joy and suffering" do not carry the same poetry as "well and woe." Which brings me to an important disclosure: as a translator, the beauty of language is as important to me as the discursive content. I don't just want my translations to be "true"; I want them to be beautiful—a pleasure to read, a heart-opening encounter. Julian also refers to union with God as "oneing." Isn't that beautiful? The soul longs to be "one-ed" with God, and he wants nothing more than to "one" himself with her.

Now to the more complex theological issue of "sin" in Julian's writings. Throughout the text she grapples with a paradox. Her "showings" revealed that sin is "no-thing," and yet she sees ample evidence of the harm caused by the human impulse to initiate and experience suffering. In keeping with the Hebrew roots of the verb, I generally translate "to sin" as "to miss the mark." For sin as a noun, I alternately use "error," "transgression," "imperfection," and "negativity." For the concept of "salvation," I offer the more Eastern notion of "liberation." The Savior becomes the Liberator.

Still, translating classic mystical masterpieces is a delicate undertaking. It is a dance between fidelity to the original and accessibility for a new audience. I want to make a place at Julian's table for people of all faiths and none, without offending those of her own root tradition. As a translator of the Christian mystics, I must continuously check my impulse to change some of my subject's more dogmatic notions to suit my own interspiritual sensibilities. I let Jesus be Jesus. I do not take it upon myself to strip the Roman Church of its authority. Catholicism was the only spiritual flavor available to Julian of Norwich in her time and place. This was the home in which the Holy One visited her. From there, he took her hand and led her out into the wild places of spirit where all mystics travel—a place that has no map and transcends all description.

I hope that Julian of Norwich would bless this translation of the *Revelations of Divine Love* as faithful to the original. I certainly felt her presence every time I sat down at my desk, lit a candle, and called on her to guide me as I endeavored to untangle, reweave, and restore the vitality of her wisdom for my "fellow spiritual seekers."

For those curious about the original Middle English text, I encourage you to get your hands on a copy and compare them. Julian was a contemporary of Chaucer, and the first woman to write in English. It is well worth the effort to read her in her native voice. I used as my source *The Showings of Julian of Norwich*, edited by Denise N. Baker, published by Norton (2005).

Part I

Revelation of Love

CHAPTER 1

Sixteen Showings of Love

This is a revelation of love that Jesus Christ, our unending bliss, gave to me in sixteen showings.

The first showing revealed his crown of thorns. This showing described the Trinity in detail, as well as the Incarnation, and the essential unity between the human soul and the Divine. I received many beautiful revelations of love and teachings of boundless wisdom here. All the showings that followed are rooted and connected in this first one.

The second showing revealed the darkening of his lovely face, which symbolized his supreme passion.

The third showing revealed that our God—who is almighty and all-loving and the embodiment of wisdom—created all that exists and is the cause of everything that happens.

The fourth showing revealed the lashing of his tender body and the copious blood he shed.

The fifth showing revealed that the precious passion of Christ overcomes the spirit of evil.

The sixth showing revealed that our God rewards all his blessed servants with profound gratitude in the world to come.

The seventh showing revealed that both joy and suffering are bound up with the human experience. When we are illumined by grace and touched with well-being, we believe that our joy will never end. When the sadness and weariness of life descends on us, we are tempted to believe that this, too, is endless. But we take refuge in a deep inner knowing that just as God's love uplifts us in joy, it protects us in sorrow.

The eighth showing revealed the final sufferings of Christ and his cruel death.

The ninth showing revealed that the outcome of Christ's terrible passion and heartrending death is the pure delight that infuses the blessed Trinity. He wants us to take comfort in this and be happy with him, until the time comes when all things are made clear to us in heaven.

The tenth showing revealed that the heart of our Lord Jesus has been broken in two for love.

The eleventh showing was an exalted revelation of his blessed Mother.

The twelfth showing revealed that our Lord is the supreme source of all life.

The thirteenth showing revealed that our God wants us to deeply appreciate the magnificence of what he has done and truly cherish all that he has made, especially the excellence of human life—since he placed human beings in charge of all creation—and acknowledge the precious amends he made for our shortcomings. He transformed all our blame into everlasting honor. In this showing he said, "Behold! By the same power, wisdom, and goodness that I have done all this, I shall make well all that is not well. You will see this for yourself." He also revealed that he wants us to have faith in his holy community and not demand that he disclose all his secrets now, but trust that we will know whatever we need to know in this life.

The fourteenth showing revealed that God is the ground of all our seeking. Two great things are contained in this single truth: one is the perfection of prayer; the other is the importance of faith. In this way, our prayer becomes his joy, and the emptiness of our longing is filled with his goodness.

The fifteenth showing revealed that one day all our pain and sorrow will be lifted and his goodness will deliver us to a place where he will offer himself as our reward and we shall live with him in everlasting bliss.

The sixteenth showing revealed that the Creator, in the form of the blessed Trinity and contained within our redeemer, Christ Jesus, eternally dwells in our souls. From this place, he righteously rules over all things, rescuing and protecting us with his wisdom and power. For the sake of love, he prevents us from succumbing to the spirit of evil.

CHAPTER 2

Three Wishes

These showings were revealed on May 8, 1373, to a simple, unlearned creature, who had once asked for three gifts from God: one, participation in his passion; two, a life-threatening illness; and three, the grace of the triple-wound (contrition, compassion, and unbearable longing).

I already believed that my devotion had given me a real sense of Christ's passion, yet I aspired (by the grace of God) to know it more deeply. I had this intense desire to go back in time and live with Mary Magdalene and with all Christ's other lovers. But, since this was not possible, I prayed instead for a vision that would give me some experience of the suffering of our Savior and of the compassion of his blessed Mother and of all his true lovers who witnessed his pain. I wanted to be one of them, to suffer alongside them. All I hoped for was to have a deeper awareness of Christ after this vision. I did not ask to be shown anything else beyond this until the time came that my soul left my body (I had faith that God's mercy would one day reveal everything).

The second gift came to my mind effortlessly: I freely wished for the grace of a serious illness. I wanted the disease to be so severe that I would believe I was dying and all the creatures who witnessed my suffering would think so too and would arrange for me to receive all the holy rites of the religious community. I had no desire for the comforts of earthly life. Rather, I yearned to fully experience all the discomfort of dying—physical and mental—with the accompanying terror and temptations of the spirits of evil. I wished to go to the brink of death, but not pass over. What I wanted was for this sickness to purify me, so that, by the grace of God, I would live more fully for his sake alone. Also, I was hoping it would prepare me for my real death, which I anticipated would soon be coming. I was ready to return to my God and Maker.

I suspected that these two desires—to share in Christ's passion and to endure a serious illness—were not exactly customary prayers, so I tempered my petitions like this: *Lord, you know what I want. If it be thy will, please give it to me. If it be not thy will, Good Lord, please do not be displeased with me, for I want nothing except that thy will be done.*

Unlike the first two prayers, my third wish was unconditional: to receive the triple-wound of a humble heart, kind compassion, and all-consuming longing for God. This third desire was so powerful that I left out the "if it be thy will" part. The first two prayers soon passed from my mind, while the third prayer perpetually burned in my heart.

CHAPTER 3

As I Lay Dying

When I was thirty and a half years old, God sent me that illness I had asked for in my youth. For three days and three nights I lay in my bed, and on the fourth night I was given the last rites of Holy Church. No one expected me to live through the night, yet I lingered for another two days. I kept thinking I was about to die, and everyone who sat with me thought so also.

I was still young enough to be sad about dying. It's not that anything here on earth pleased me (it did not), or that I was afraid of pain (I trusted in his mercy). Rather, I would have liked to live longer simply so that I could have learned to love God better. I thought that if I had more time to practice loving God, I could take this knowledge with me into the bliss of the world to come. It suddenly seemed to me that my time here on earth had been so short in comparison to life everlasting that it hardly counted at all.

This made me think, *Good Lord, could it be that my living is no longer to your glory?*

The pain in my body, combined with my own common sense, led me to conclude that yes, my life was over. And so I assented with all the will of my heart to be completely aligned with God's will. I remained in this state until daybreak. By then my body was dead from the waist down. I couldn't feel a thing. The people who were with me propped my body up in bed, so that I could align my heart to God's will, and so that I could more easily think of him as my life ebbed away. Someone sent for the parish priest to be with me when I died. By the time he arrived, my eyes had rolled back in my head and I could no longer speak.

Sharing His Suffering

The priest placed a crucifix in front of my face and said, "I have brought the image of your savior. Gaze upon it and draw comfort from it."

I thought I was all right just the way I was—with my eyes turned upward toward heaven where I trusted I was heading—but I consented to force my eyes to rest on the crucifix and discovered that it was actually easier to endure looking straight ahead than up. That's when my sight began to fail. Everything grew dim, until the whole room was as dark as night. The only thing I could see was the cross, which was bathed in a rather ordinary light. I couldn't figure out how it was possible that only this single object was illuminated. Everything except the cross looked ugly to me, as if it were all tainted by demons.

After this, the upper part of my body began to die. Soon I had almost no feeling left. The worst part was my shortness of breath and the sense that my life was rapidly waning. By this time I was convinced that I was passing away. Suddenly all my pain vanished, and I was whole again. In fact, I felt better than I ever had before—especially in the center part of my body. This abrupt transformation astonished me. It seemed to me that it was the work of the Divine and not something natural. But, in spite of the all-pervading comfort I was feeling, I had no confidence that

I would survive. I was not fully at ease, because my heart was set on being set free from this world.

All at once it came into my mind that this would be a good time to ask God for the second wound: that my body become a vessel for Christ's blessed passion. Remember? I had once wished that his pains could be my pains and that my heart would fill with compassion and then burn with longing for God. I thought that I was finally ready to receive the grace of the triple-wound I had asked for.

I did not desire any kind of physical vision or revelation from God. All I wanted was the kind of compassion that naturally flows into the soul in response to the suffering of our Lord, who for the sake of love agreed to incarnate as a mortal man. I wished to suffer along with him, inside my own human body, if God would only give me the grace to do so.

CHAPTER 4

Encountering the Trinity

All of a sudden, I saw the red blood trickling down from under his garland of thorns. The blood flowed hot and fresh, just as abundantly as it had during the time of his passion when the actual thorns pressed into his blessed head. As I watched, I realized that it was Christ himself who was showing this vision to me—he who was both God and man, who suffered like this for me—and that he was revealing himself directly, without anyone or anything between us.

In the midst of this showing the blessed Trinity also revealed itself to me and filled my heart to overflowing with joy. I realized that this is what it will be like in the world to come, for all beings, and for all time. For the Trinity is God, and God is the Trinity. The Trinity is our creator and our sustainer, our Beloved forever and ever, our endless joy and bliss. I saw all this in the first revelation and in every showing after that. Whenever Christ appeared, I seemed to understand the blessed Trinity, as well.

"*Benedicte domine!*" I cried. "Blessed be the Lord!" I said, in a full voice, with reverence and intention, in awe and amazement. I was thoroughly astonished that he who is so great—so holy and majestic—would bother to mingle with such a homely creature as

I. What I realized was that our Lord Jesus Christ, moved by loving compassion (and with the permission and protection of God), wanted to bolster me with his comfort so that I could face all my demons before I died. This sight of his blessed passion, combined with the revelation of the Godhead in my understanding, helped me to believe that I had the strength to overcome whatever spirits of evil and other supernatural temptations I might encounter.

Saint Mary

Next, he brought our blessed Mother, Saint Mary, to my mind. I saw her spiritually, and also in form. She was very young—a simple, humble girl—barely older than a child. She appeared as the same size and age that she was in real life when she conceived the Christ Child. God showed me some of the wisdom and truth of her soul, and I understood the contemplative reverence with which she beheld her God and maker, the awe and wonder she experienced when she discovered that he had chosen her, a modest creature of his own creation, to be a vessel for the Divine.

From this place of wisdom and truth, fully aware of God's vastness and of her own littleness, both humbly and boldly, she responded to the angel Gabriel, "Behold! Here I am, the handmaiden of God."

In this showing I came to understand that she exceeds the grace and worth of all God's creatures. There is no one greater than Mary, except (in my opinion) the blessed humanity of Christ.

CHAPTER 5

A Hazelnut

At the same time as I saw the bleeding head, our good Lord gave me a spiritual vision of his simple loving. I saw that he is everything that is good for us, everything that soothes and helps us. He is our clothing; he wraps himself around us, enfolding us in his love. His tender love is our shelter; he will never leave us.

Then he showed me a small thing, the size of a hazelnut, nestled in the palm of my hand. It was round as a ball. I looked at it with the eyes of my understanding and thought, *What can this be?* And the answer came to me: *It is all that is created.* I was amazed that it could continue to exist. It seemed to me to be so little that it was on the verge of dissolving into nothingness. And then these words entered my understanding: *It lasts, and will last forever, because God loves it. Everything that is has its being through the love of God.*

I saw three attributes of this small thing: the first is that God made it; the second is that he loves it; and the third that he sustains it. But what did I behold in that? Well, I saw the creator, the lover, and the sustainer. And I recognized that until I am completely one with him I shall never have deep rest nor full joy. No, not until I am so thoroughly oned to him that no created thing can come between my God and myself. Such a tiny object stood for all creation! I became aware that we should dismiss as nothing all that is created, so that we can we can fully receive and adore our uncreated God.

He Is Enough

This is the reason why our hearts and souls are not at perfect ease. We seek refuge in small things, but cannot find comfort there. We do not recognize our God who is all-powerful, all-wise, and all-good. He is our only true rest. And he wishes to be known. He wants us to rest in him. He is all that is, and he knows that anything less is not enough for us. This is why no soul can find peace until it empties itself of all forms. Only when the soul has willingly become nothing, out for love of him who is everything, can it find true rest.

Our Lord also showed me that it gives him great pleasure when a simple soul comes to him naked, open, and intimate. This is an expression of the love-longing awakened in the soul that has been touched by the Holy Spirit. I understood this when the following prayer came to me: *God, through your goodness, give me yourself. You are enough for me. I cannot honor you by asking for anything less. When I do ask for less, I am never satisfied. Only in you do I have all.*

These words praise the absolute goodness of God and are very dear to the soul. They come close to touching upon the truth of the divine will. God's goodness floods creation, infusing all of his blessed works, endlessly overflowing all that is, for he is everlastingness. He made us for himself alone. He restored us through his blessed passion. He sustains us always in his perfect love. And all this flows from his goodness.

CHAPTER 6

Intermediaries

The aim of this showing was to teach our soul to cherish God's goodness above all else. This made me reflect on the habitual ways we may have learned to pray. Because we do not really understand the nature of love, we create a multitude of intermediaries that stand between our souls and our Beloved.

I realized that we honor God much more truly and joyfully when we pray to him directly than if we were to employ all the intermediaries the heart can think of. Then, if our understanding is clear and our belief steadfast, we will cleave to his goodness and be held there. There is not an intermediary we can invent that would come close to fully honoring God. All that we could ever wish is contained in his fullness. Anything less is too little.

This is what came to my mind next: We pray to God in the form of Christ's holy flesh and precious blood, his holy passion and glorious wounds and precious death, his blessed humanity and the everlasting life it offers us, but all this unfolds from his formless goodness. We pray to God in the form of the sweet mother who bore Christ and the love she embodies, but all the help we receive from her arises from his formless goodness. We pray to God in the form of the holy cross Christ died on, but all the strength and hope we draw from this is rooted in his formless goodness. We pray to God by calling on special saints and the circle of heavenly beings who offer us precious love and endless friendship, but everything we receive from them has its source in his formless goodness. The multitude of intermediaries we call upon for spiritual assistance are ordained by God and are beautiful and worthy. The most wondrous intermediary of all is his blessed humanity, which came through the vessel of the maiden. All intermediaries flow from God's wellspring of formless goodness. They all contribute to our atonement and our liberation.

And so it is not wrong to seek God and praise him through his intermediaries, as long as we remember that he is the goodness within everything. For the highest prayer possible is the goodness of God, and it infuses our lowest needs. It vitalizes our souls and makes them burst into life. It makes us grow in virtue and flourish in grace. It is closest to our own true nature and swift in its blessing. It is the grace of God's goodness that our souls seek and always will, until we come to know God directly and realize that he already has us enfolded in himself.

The Miracle of the Human Body

God does not disdain anything he has created. Human beings walk upright, and the food we eat is elegantly stored in our body, like money secured in a purse. When the time comes, the body opens, releases what it no longer needs, and is sealed back up again. Just like that! It is clear that it is God who has devised this perfect system. Didn't he tell us that he comes to us in our humblest needs? For love of our souls, which he made in his own likeness, he lovingly serves us in our most basic bodily functions.

The body is held in its clothes, the flesh in the skin, the bones in the flesh, and the heart in the breast. So are we—body and soul—draped and contained in the goodness of God. Even more intimately than that! Because the body wears down and wastes away, but the goodness of God is always whole and immediately available. All that our Beloved wants is for us to hold to his goodness with all our might and forevermore. Nothing our heart can conceive of could possibly please God as fully as this or yield more powerful results.

God's love for us is so great that it surpasses the understanding of any living being. Not a creature in all of creation can know how completely and how sweetly and with what infinite tenderness he loves us. Only with his grace and his assistance can we persevere in spiritual contemplation and maintain the awe and wonder that arise in our hearts in response to the soaring, transcendent, immeasurable love that the almighty God, in his goodness, has for us.

And so we can approach our Beloved with great devotion, asking for our hearts' deepest desire, knowing that what we really want is God, and that all God really wants is us. This love-longing will continue to burn in our hearts until we possess him in the fullness of joy. Then there will be nothing left to yearn for. God will fully occupy us in knowing him and loving him, until we leave this world and are completely fulfilled in the world to come.

This lesson of love became the foundation of all the showings that were to come. Contemplation of God's love gives the soul perspective. In light of this vastness, we behold our own littleness, and this fills us with awe and humility. It also awakens in us abundant love for all our fellow beings.

CHAPTER 7

Herring Scales

To help me learn the meaning of this revelation, our Beloved showed me Our Lady Saint Mary. I recognized that she is the embodiment of exalted wisdom and truth. When Mary encountered her creator, she could not help but contemplate his soaring grandeur and his mighty goodness. The greatness and nobility of her vision of God filled her with awe and devotion. She saw herself as nothing compared to her Beloved—so simple and so little—which infused her with humility. This is why Mary is full of grace and overflows with all kinds of virtues and surpasses all creatures.

At the same time that I beheld Mary in a spiritual vision, I was watching the copious bleeding of Christ's head in a bodily vision. Huge drops of blood fell from beneath his garland like globes. They were thick and round, and seemed to be flowing directly from his veins. As they emerged they were a reddish-brown color, and when they spread out, they turned bright red. The blood vanished when it reached his eyebrows. Yet somehow he kept bleeding, and as he did, many things were revealed to me. The beauty and vitality of the vision continued to unfold. I couldn't possibly compare this to anything but itself!

Nevertheless, three images came to mind at the same time: one was the roundness of the drops of blood as they emerged from his head; another was way the drops looked like the scales of a herring as they spread over his forehead; and the other was that the flow was so abundant it reminded me of rain cascading from the eaves of a house. This showing was vivid and alive, hideous and dreadful, and sweet and lovely.

Our Friendly Lord

Of all the showings revealed to me, the one that gave me the most comfort was that our sweet Lord—who is infinitely exalted and alone is worthy of worship—is also utterly simple and friendly. This realization filled me to overflowing with feelings of delight and soul-safety. To help me understand this, he gave me a clear example. The highest honor a person of power can give to a less powerful person is friendliness, especially when he enthusiastically demonstrates his affection, both in private and in public. This makes the less powerful person think, *Oh! How could such a noble being honor me any more completely and give me any greater joy than to share with me (who is so ordinary) his personal friendship? This means far more to me than if he were to lavish me with expensive gifts but treat me in a cold and distant manner.*

This showing was so vivid and uplifting, it ravished my heart, and in light of his tender intimacy, I lost myself in joy and almost forgot who I was altogether. That's how it is with our sweet Lord. The one who is highest and mightiest, most noble and honorable, is also nearest and gentlest, most humble and accessible. Someday we shall all see him face-to-face, and he will personally manifest his friendship to each one of us. Our Beloved wants us to believe this with all our hearts—to trust in this and rejoice in it—and use this promise to console ourselves as best we can, with his grace and his help, until the time comes when we experience it for ourselves.

As I see it, the greatest blessing we could ever receive is this wonderful courtesy and familiarity from our Father, who is our Creator, through our sweet Jesus Christ, who is our Brother and our Savior. It's almost impossible to become aware of this sacred friendship in this life, unless it is given to us through a special showing from our sweet Lord or through an abundant flow of grace with which the Holy Spirit fills us from within. But when we ground our lives in faith, hope, and love, we make ourselves ready to receive this gift. The rest is a matter of grace.

God reveals his sacred friendship to whomever he wills. He directly imparts many secret details that our faith told us about, all of which celebrate his glory. Once such a revelation has passed—and it only lasts a short time—our faith keeps it alive (by the grace of the Holy Spirit) for the rest of our lives. And so this showing reveals nothing less or more than our faith has already taught us, only now we know it with the whole of our souls.

CHAPTER 8

Not for Me Alone

Throughout the duration of this showing, I couldn't help uttering these words: *Benedicte domine* (Blessed be the Lord)! I gleaned six things from the revelation of the abundant bleeding of his dear head. First, his precious blood is a token of his sacred passion. Second, the sweet maiden is his blessed mother. Third, the holy Godhead always was, is, and shall be; it is All-Power, All-Wisdom, All-Love. Fourth, God made all that is. I know that heaven and earth and the whole of creation are ample and generous, beautiful and good, but it all appeared so small to me in my vision because I was in the Presence of the creator of all things, and to a soul that sees the creator of everything the creation itself seems very little by comparison. Fifth, he made everything for love, and by love all things are sustained and protected, and ever shall be. Sixth, God is everything that is good; the goodness in everything is God.

This is what the Beloved showed me in the first revelation, and he gave me time and space to contemplate it. The bodily vision faded, but the spiritual insight seeped into my understanding. I waited with awe and devotion, rejoicing in what I saw. As much as I dared, I wished to see even more, or at least more of the same

21

for a longer time. I was moved by a deep love for my fellow spiritual seekers, praying that they could all see what I was seeing, because I knew it would be such a comfort to them. I understood that the vision I was receiving was not for me alone, but for all beings.

Today Is My Judgment Day

Then I said to those around me, "Today is my judgment day." I said this because I expected to die, and I had been taught that when men and women die they have to make an accounting of their lives and accept the eternal consequences of their actions. I wanted the people around me to realize that life is short and to use my example to love God better. I was preparing for my death, but I was torn. On the one hand, I was lost in wonderment; on the other, I was sad, because it seemed that my vision imparted teachings meant for the living.

Everything I say about myself here I mean to apply to all spiritual seekers, for God has made it clear to me that he gave me these showings for the good of everyone. And so I implore you for God's sake, and I advise you for your own benefit, to disregard the humble servant to whom this revelation was shown and direct your attention to the One who revealed it. Contemplate your Beloved with all your heart and all your mind and all your strength. In his gracious love and goodness, he desires that this vision be of comfort to us all.

CHAPTER 9

Loving God Better

This revelation does not make me a better person. I am only better if I love God better. And if it makes you love God better, the vision is more for you than for me. I am not saying this to those of you who are wise, for you already know it well. But as for those who are simple, like me, you may draw comfort and strength from this account. We are all one in love.

It is clear to me that God does not favor me above the simplest soul who dwells in a state of grace. I am sure there are many people who have never had visions and yet love God far better than I do. When I look at myself as an individual, I see that I am nothing. It is only in unity with my fellow spiritual seekers that I am anything at all. It is this foundation of unity that will save humanity.

Loving All That Is

God is all that is good. God has created all that is made. God loves all that he has created. And so anyone who, in loving God, loves all his fellow creatures loves all that is. All those who are on the spiritual path contain the whole of creation, and the Creator. That is because God is inside us, and inside God is everything. And so whoever loves God loves all that is. I sincerely pray that whoever needs to hear this hears it and draws deep comfort from it.

I speak about those who will be saved because at the time of my vision God did not show me anything about the rest of humanity. I try to conform to the teachings of my faith tradition and not to deviate from them. I do hope, by the grace of God, that I kept the beliefs I held before these revelations close to me throughout the showings. I would not have presumed to say or do anything contrary to the teachings of the Church! And so, with this intention, I diligently contemplated my visions and never experienced anything I beheld as being in conflict with my religion.

These showings came in three ways: as physical sights, as words formed in my understanding, and by spiritual vision. I neither know nor could I possibly explain how this last kind of vision occurred, so all I can do is trust in our Beloved, in his goodness, to show it to you himself. He can give you this understanding more directly and more sweetly than I could ever convey with my words.

CHAPTER 10

His Ravaged Face

Next, I had a physical vision of the face on the crucifix. As I stared at it, the face began to shift and change. I beheld aspects of his passion: vile contempt, spitting and pummeling, and more excruciating wounds than I could possibly count. And the face kept changing color. At one point I saw that half the face was thickly caked with dried blood from the ear to the nose. Then the blood vanished from one side and appeared on the other. Then it disappeared from both sides. This vision was physical, but dim, and it filled my heart with sorrow. I wished for more light, so I could more clearly see what was going on.

But no sooner did I have this desire than a voice spoke in my mind: *If God wants to show you more, he will be your light. You need no other light than him.* There I was, seeing him and seeking him at the same time! We are so blind, so foolish. We do not start seeking God until he begins to show himself to us. Then, when he reveals a glimpse of himself to us, through his grace, that same grace inspires us to strive to see him more perfectly. In this way I saw him and I looked for him; I had him and I longed for him. As I see it, this is the way things are, and the way things ought to be.

Plunging into the Sea

At some point, my mind was plunged into the depths of the sea. I saw green hills and valleys, which seemed to be covered in tiny pebbles, strewn with seaweed and moss. What I realized was that even if a man or a woman were brought down to the bottom of the ocean each could still see God. This is because there is nowhere where God is not. Not only is God everywhere, but he keeps us safe and protected from harm wherever we are. When we see God, we have more strength and comfort than we can possibly describe with the language of this world. We believe that we hardly see God at all, but what he desires is for us to believe that we see him continuously. It is through this belief that we receive his grace. He wishes to be seen and to be sought. He wants us to yearn for him and to trust in him.

This second showing was deeply distressing. It was so small, so simple and humble, and yet it filled my soul with sorrow and longing. It also terrified me. There were moments when I doubted that it really was a vision from God. And then our sweet Lord would give me new insights, and I would be reassured that it truly was a divine revelation.

Veronica's Veil

This showing symbolized the shame of our negative deeds, which our sweet, bright, blessed Lord bore for us. It made me think of the veil of the blessed Veronica, which carried the imprint of his holy face as he was in the throes of his cruel passion, willingly bound for his death. This cloth has often changed color, from brownish to blackish, causing many people to marvel and wonder at the mystery. How did the image get there? And why is the image imprinted there so discolored, so ravaged and miserable?

The true face of the one reflected in Veronica's veil was the very essence of the beauty of heaven, flower of the earth, fruit of the blessed maiden's womb. Here is what I understood about this, by the grace of God.

Our faith teaches us that the entire Trinity created human beings in its image. We also know that when we fell so far from grace our only help came from the One who created us. We must also understand that the One who created us for love restores us through love, lifting us to an even higher state of bliss than we experienced before our fall. Just as we were made in the likeness of the Trinity the first time we were created, our Maker wishes us to be like Christ our Savior, dwelling forever and ever in a state of grace, by the power of our re-creation. Because of his love for humanity, he was willing to make himself as much like a man as possible, experiencing all the misery and wretchedness of the human condition, only free from sin.

This is how we may understand the significance of this showing. Remember how I said before that our bright and lovely Lord concealed his Godhead inside our pale and lowly flesh? Now I dare to say—and you must dare to believe—that there was never a human being alive as beautiful as he was. Not even when his tender face was transfigured by suffering, darkened with his dying, not even when he collapsed under the weight of his toil, was his glory diminished.

He Wants Us to Seek Him

The main lesson I learned from this showing is that God loves it when we seek him. The Holy Spirit fills us with longing, and all we can do is seek, suffer, and surrender. Then, when it is God's will, what we seek is illuminated with perfect clarity, and we find it. This is grace. What pleases God is our continual search, fueled

27

by faith, hope, and love. What pleases us is encountering the object of our heart's deepest desire, which fills us with joy. And so this is what I came to understand: During the time when it is God's will for the soul to struggle and strive, seeking is as good as finding. God wants us to seek him with all our might until we find him, and when he shows himself to us at last, it is by his special grace.

God himself will teach the soul how to bear this encounter. He will show us what most deeply honors him and what most powerfully benefits us. The grace and guidance of the Holy Spirit will instill in us the humility and other virtues required for this blessing. Whether the soul is in a state of seeking or finding, the way we honor God most is through unconditional surrender. With his grace, and bolstered by the moral discernment taught by our faith tradition, every soul has a right to both seek and behold the Beloved.

So, to sum up these teachings, it is God's will that we strive for three things: The first is willingness. We must seek with diligence, without laziness, and, as much as possible and by his grace, gladly and joyfully, unencumbered by unreasonable sadness or useless depression. The second is patience. We should be steadfast as we wait for him, secure in his love, without grumbling or pushing against him, even if it takes a whole lifetime, because the truth is this life is much shorter than we think. Finally, complete faith. We need to actively trust him, knowing that he is likely to appear suddenly and without warning, raining blessings upon all his lovers. Although he works in secret, he desires to be perceived. And although he appears when we least expect it, he wants to be trusted. He really is simple, friendly, and utterly gracious.

May he be forever blessed!

CHAPTER 11

A Single Point

Next, I saw God in a single point in my mind. I contemplated this point with my full attention and realized that God is the center of all that is and the Doer of all that is done. With tender awe, I pondered this realization. Then, this question arose in my mind: *What is sin?*

For I saw truly that God is responsible for everything, no matter how little, and nothing happens by luck or chance. Everything is guided by the all-seeing wisdom of God. If we view things as happening by accident, it is because we lack divine sight. In God's all-seeing wisdom, all things have their rightful place since before the beginning of time. He brings everything, always, to its perfect conclusion. Since some things seem to us to come out of nowhere and catch us unaware, our natural lack of omniscience makes us think that they are a matter of bad luck or happy chance.

This revelation of love compelled me to conclude that all that is done is well done, for our sweet Lord is the Doer.

At this time, I was not shown the work of creatures, but only the work of the Creator. What I saw was that he is the midpoint of all, and he does everything and is incapable of sin. This led me to believe that sin is *no thing*. Nowhere in all that was revealed to me did I see a trace of sin. And so I stopped looking for it and moved on, placing myself in God's hand, allowing him to show me what he wanted me to see.

Rightfulness

What I saw next was the absolute rightfulness of God's action for all souls. Rightfulness has two beautiful aspects: it is right, and it is full. And so are all the actions of our sweet Lord. Nothing he does ever lacks mercy or grace. Everything he does is right-full. Nothing is missing. Later, God would show me another vision in which I saw sin in all its nakedness, and I had to contemplate this. Yet even here what was most clear to me was his unconditional mercy and grace.

Our Beloved revealed this vision to me because he truly wants to turn our souls toward him, to contemplate him and his wonderful works. All his judgments are gentle and sweet. Once a soul stops paying attention to the blind opinions of humanity and focuses instead on the gracious consideration of the Divine, it finds the comfort it has been yearning for. Human beings deem certain actions as good and others as evil, but this is not the way our Lord sees things. God created everything that exists in nature, and he is the force behind everything that happens.

It's easy enough to see that the best deeds are well done. But we must also understand that the most insignificant acts are just as important as the most exalted, because they all share the common trait of being ordained by the Divine. He places all things in their rightful order, since before time began, for there is no Doer but he.

Perfectly Arranged

What I saw was that he never changes his divine purpose in anything and never shall for all eternity. He has arranged everything perfectly, and nothing is unknown to him. In fact, he put everything in order before anything was even created! He made all things for the highest good, to endure forever, and not a single thing will ever fall short of that mark.

This is why the blessed Trinity is always completely happy with everything he does. God has revealed all this with abundant blessing, as if to say, *See, I am God! See, I am inside everything and I do everything. See my hand in all my works: I shall never lift it, for all eternity. See, I guide all things to the goal I ordained for them, by the same power, wisdom, and love with which I created them. How could anything possibly be amiss?*

And so my soul was powerfully, wisely, and lovingly tested through this showing. I came to know that my task is to assent to God's will with reverence and rejoice in all his works.

CHAPTER 12

Dearworthy Blood

As I watched, his body continued to bleed profusely, which is to be expected from the scourging he endured. The vicious blows split the tender flesh of his lovely body in deep fissures. The hot blood was so copious that I couldn't even see the wounds from which it emerged or the skin over which it flowed. It was all blood, everywhere. When it came to the point where the blood should have fallen, it vanished. And yet it kept flowing, and I kept watching. The bleeding was so profuse that it seemed to me that, if this had been happening in the physical world rather than in a vision, the blood would have soaked my bed and overflowed onto the floor, splashing up the sides of the walls.

Then it occurred to me that, in his tender love for all creatures, God created bountiful waters on earth for our use and our comfort. Yet it pleases him even more when we accept the precious blood he offers to cleanse our spiritual impurities. There is no liquid in creation he would rather share with us. By virtue of his blessed Godhead, it is boundless and infinitely precious. This blood is an aspect of our own nature, and it flows from his generous love.

The dearworthy blood of our sweet Lord is as plentiful as it is sacred. Behold and see! The precious bounty descended to the depths of hell and burst the bonds that ensnared all beings there, lifting them to the holy halls of paradise. The precious bounty flows over the whole of the earth, bathing all beings in grace, swiftly cleansing the impurities of every creature of goodwill, now and forever. The precious bounty ascended to the heights of heaven and merged with the blessed body of our Lord, where it continues to circulate inside him, and he keeps bleeding and praying on our behalf to the Creator of all that is, for as long as we need it. It flows and flows, throughout every level of paradise, rejoicing in the liberation of the whole of humanity, until we reach our final number and are all set free.

CHAPTER 13

No Wrath in God

Before God revealed any words to me, he allowed me to simply gaze upon him for a long time. I contemplated all that I had seen, and to the extent that my simple soul could understand it, I pondered its meaning. Then, without a voice or opening his lips, he said to my soul, *In this way, the spirit of evil is overcome.* What he meant was that the power of his blessed passion is greater than all darkness. The Adversary is wicked, but he's impotent.

God showed me that the spirit of evil has not changed since before the incarnation. He harbors just as much malice, he works just has hard to entrap us, but all he sees is that, through Christ's precious passion, we slip out of his grasp again and again. That is the Adversary's sorrow. All God permits him to do turns into joy for us and pain and shame for him. He suffers just as much when God allows him to do his work as when he does not. He can never cause as much damage as he would like, because all his power is locked in God's hand.

Remember: there can be no wrath in God. He endlessly upholds that which honors him and, with infinite power and perfect justice, opposes the forces of evil, which busily conspire to act against the divine will.

Laughter

I saw Christ scorn the malice of the Adversary and thoroughly dismiss him as powerless, and I saw that he wants us to discount him, too. This made me laugh out loud, which made the people around me laugh. Their laughter brought me great delight. I thought, *I wish all my fellow seekers could see what I have seen and laugh with me.* Even though Christ himself, I noticed, was not laughing, I was well aware that he showed me that sight to make me laugh. When we see that the power of love overcomes the spirit of evil, it fills our hearts with comfort and joy. As I focused my attention on my Lord, he revealed an inner understanding of his unchanging truth, and his outward expression remained constant. As I see it, constancy is one of the divine attributes. His truth endures forever.

After this bout of mirth, I fell back into sobriety. "I see three things," I said. "Amusement, scorn, and seriousness. It amuses me that the Lord of Love overcomes the spirit of evil. I realize that God sees evil for what it is, and scorns it, and always will. And it strikes me as extremely serious that Christ paid for this triumph with his blessed passion, with clear intention and heavy labor."

God showed me that the spirit of evil is damned. I saw that, in the end, all those who will be liberated will dismiss him, and their liberation will fill him with envy. Then he will see that all the sorrow and tribulation he caused them has been transformed into everlasting joy. All the pain and woe he wanted to bring them will be swallowed with him in the darkness forever.

CHAPTER 14

Everyone Is Welcome

Then our sweet Lord said to me, "Thank you for working so hard and serving me with such dedication when you were young."

These words transported me to paradise. I envisioned our Beloved as a nobleman who has invited all his dearest friends to his magnificent home for a feast. I saw that he did not claim any special seat for himself at the table, but rather entertained everyone there, filling the house with laughter and joy. With his simple friendship he brought tremendous gladness and deep comfort to all his guests. His own blessed countenance radiated endless love and emanated the sublimest melody. It is this same face of the Godhead that fills up the heavens with divine bliss.

Three Degrees of Bliss

At this point, God revealed to me three degrees of bliss that everyone who has ever served him in even the smallest degree on earth shall enjoy for all eternity. The first is that once we are delivered from the pain of this world, God will pour his loving gratitude on us. This blessing is such a profound honor that the soul feels itself completely filled and cannot possibly wish for anything more. I could not imagine that all the suffering and hard work any one of us has willingly endured here on earth for his sake is worthy of such exalted recognition by our Beloved.

The second degree of bliss is that he will give us thanks in front of all the blessed beings that dwell in paradise. They will each bear witness to God's gratitude for our particular service. Then an example of this occurred to me. When a king thanks his servants, it does them great honor. When he expresses his gratitude in the presence of the whole realm, the servant's honor is vastly increased.

The third degree of bliss is that, as delicious as the divine gratitude feels in the moment, it shall last forever and ever. I saw also (simply and sweetly) that it does not matter what age a person was when she offered herself in service to the Divine. For even one day of willing service, even at the very end of a long life, is enough to earn every soul all three degrees of bliss. And yet he is especially grateful for those who offered themselves to him from a young age. Those who give their youth to him are wonderfully thanked and rewarded accordingly.

The more we understand the graciousness of our God, the happier we are to lovingly serve him all the days of our lives.

CHAPTER 15

Shifting Between Certainty and Despair

Next, he revealed the most exquisite pleasure within my own soul. I was filled with everlasting certainty, which pervaded my being with its sustaining power and drove out all pain and fear. What a welcome feeling! It was so joyful and so spiritual that I was brought into a state of complete peace, ease, and stillness. There was nothing on earth that could have grieved me.

This lasted only a little while, however. Then the feeling shifted, and I was plunged into the depths of despair. I felt abandoned. I was so weary of my life, so annoyed with myself that I barely had the patience to go on living. I felt that there was no relief or comfort for me anywhere but in the stubborn clinging to faith, hope, and love. And so I clung to these truths, but I did not *feel* them.

Then, all of a sudden, God gave me comfort and joy again. My soul rested in a state of such delightful security and powerful bliss that there was no fear, no sorrow, or physical pain that could be suffered that would have bothered me. And then again I was suffering. And then I was in bliss. Back and forth—first one, then the other—maybe twenty times. In the times of joy I could have joined St. Paul in saying, "Nothing shall separate me from the love of Christ!" When I was suffering, I could have said with St. Peter, "Lord, save me; I am perishing!"

Well and Woe

What this revelation showed me is that some souls benefit from this range of feelings. Sometimes we are surrounded with the comforting presence of God; other times we feel as if we had failed and are left to ourselves. God wants us to know that he supports us equally in well and woe. But for our own benefit he sometimes leaves us alone with ourselves. This is not because we have committed any transgression. When it happened to me, I had done nothing bad enough to make God abandon me. It was very sudden. But I had not earned that wonderful blessed feeling, either. Our Beloved freely gives us joy, and sometimes he allows us to suffer. Both are one love.

It is God's will that we do everything in our power to find that inner consolation and rest in it. Pain passes, but that divine bliss is eternal. The suffering of this life will dissolve into nothing. For those who love God the reward is everlasting joy. It is not God's will that we wallow in our pain and collapse in despair. Instead, we should pass through these states as lightly as possible, sustaining ourselves in the endless delight that is God.

CHAPTER 16

Changing Colors

After this, Christ gave me a glimpse of his passion, leading up to his death. I saw his sweet face turn dry and bloodless. All color had drained from it, and he was deathly pale. His face continued to grow more ashen, then faded from grey to blue, darkening to a deeper blue, and then brown. As death invaded the flesh, the skin looked increasingly lifeless.

His agony was reflected most clearly in his blessed face—especially his sweet lips. Where those lips were once vibrant, ruddy, and sensual, now I watched as they dried up and turned to darkening shades of grey, blue, brown, and black. These changes were terrible to observe, as he entered deeper into his dying. The nose, too, shriveled and collapsed. The sweet body grew brown and then black. Everything about his radiant and beautiful form dissolved into this desiccated image of death.

Bitter Wind

I saw that at the time that our Savior was dying on the cross, a dry and bitter wind was blowing. It was wondrously cold. By the time all the precious blood had been drained from his beloved body, a small amount of moisture remained in his ravaged flesh. The bloodlessness and painful drying within met with the frigid wind outside, and they converged upon the sweet body of Christ. As the hours dragged on, these four things—the anguish, the blood-loss, the wind, and the freezing cold—gradually dried up the last of his tender flesh.

Although this pain was sharp and devastating, it lasted for a very long time, slowly squeezing the vitality from every body part. I could see that this process of drying was accompanied by unbearable suffering. As long as a drop of fluid remained in Christ's sweet body, he continued to suffer. This interminable torment felt to me as if it had lasted seven days and nights. He was continuously on the verge of dying. Many times I was certain that he was suffering his final pains and was about to pass away. Indeed, the beloved body was so shriveled and discolored, it appeared as if it had already been dead for a week. It seemed to me that this drying up of Christ's flesh must be the worst and the final stage of his passion.

CHAPTER 17

Thirst

As I watched him dying, the words of Christ came to my mind, "I am thirsty." At that moment, I perceived in him a double thirst: one physical, the other spiritual. I will speak of the spiritual thirst later. The physical thirst was caused by the lack of moisture, when all his blood was drained and his blessed flesh and bones were left all alone without wetness of any kind. Abandoned, the blessed flesh was dying, drying, the nails twisting in the wounds.

The cruel hardness of the huge nails, driven deep into the tenderness of his sweet hands and feet, combined with the weight of his blessed body, made the wounds grow wider, and the flesh began to sag from hanging there for so long. The garland of thorns bit into his head, parched with dried blood, binding and chafing him. Strands of his sweet hair and pieces of desiccated flesh clung to the thorns, and the thorns embedded into the crown of his head.

When he was first nailed to the cross, and his bleeding was fresh and flowing, the continual pressure of the thorns created gaping wounds in his head. As I looked more carefully, I saw that now the sweet skin was loosening around his head. The tender flesh was scraped and broken in many places, and hung from his frame like a cloth left out to dry. The heavy, loose skin looked like it was about to fall off the bone. I was filled with sorrow and fear. I did not think I could bear to watch his flesh drop from his body. I did not see exactly how, but I understood that the violent way the crown of thorns was crushed onto his head caused terrible damage.

Crown of Thorns

This excruciating sight unfolded for quite some time, and then it began to change. I watched in horror as the drying flesh around the crown of thorns began to lose its weight and lift from his skull, forming a kind of second circle around his head, like a garland around a garland. The garland of thorns was dyed dark with his blood, and the fleshly garland was imbued with the same hue, like clotted blood after it has dried. The skin of his face and the flesh of his body were covered with fine lines, tawny in color, like a dry board of aged lumber. The face was darker than the body.

I saw four aspects to this stark aridity. One was from blood-loss. The second was the pain that accompanied this bleeding. The third was that his body was hung up in the air the way people hang out a cloth to dry. Finally, his physical nature demanded liquid, and no one would give him anything to drink or offer him comfort of any kind. Oh, such cruel and wicked suffering! It was bad enough when he was beaten and hung on the cross, but this lack of moisture, and the way it made his sweet body shrivel and collapse, was the cruelest torment of all.

Then I saw two aspects to his head pain, in particular. The first was the way the moisture inside his body began to leak away. The other was from the bitter wind that dried up his flesh from the outside. He suffered more terribly from the cold than my heart can stand to contemplate. On top of all the other pains he endured, this anguish was unimaginable. Mere words fail to describe such intolerable suffering.

My Beloved in Pain

This revelation of Christ's pain filled me to overflowing with pain. I was well aware that he had suffered once, long ago, yet he agreed to share it with me now, and it felt as if I were remembering it myself. This was just what I had asked for! I felt no pain but Christ's pain, the whole time.

Then I thought, *Little did I know what I was asking for!* Like a wretch, I regretted it. If I had realized what it really was I was praying for, I never would have had the courage to face it. My suffering went far beyond physical pain. *Is there any pain in hell equal to this?* I wondered. And then the answer came to me: *Hell is different. That is a state of despair. But of all the pains that lead to liberation, this is the greatest: to see your Beloved suffer.*

How could anything possibly cause me more pain than to witness the suffering of the one who is all my life, all my bliss, and all my joy? At that moment I was filled with an unshakable certainty: I loved Christ so much more than myself that there was no pain I could endure that would equal the suffering I experienced seeing my Beloved in pain.

CHAPTER 18

His Loving Mother

Next, I saw an aspect of the compassion of Our Lady Saint Mary. Christ and his mother were so one-ed in love that the power of her love caused the power of her pain. This helped me to realize the essence of natural love. By the grace of God, creatures have a natural love for their creator. Nowhere is this love more perfectly expressed or extravagantly revealed than in Christ's sweet mother.

Because Mary loved him more than anyone else did, her pain surpassed the pain of all the others. The higher, the more intense, the sweeter the love, the deeper the sorrow the lover feels when she sees her beloved in pain. Based on my own experience, I am certain that all Christ's disciples and true lovers suffered more harrowing pain than their own dying could ever have caused. For the least of these companions must have loved him beyond all that could possibly be said.

I saw here a powerful oneing between Christ and us, for when he is in pain, we suffer. Indeed, all created things capable of feeling pain suffer with him. At the time of Christ's death, all creation, which God made to serve us—the earth beneath us and the firmament above—failed in its natural function from sheer sorrow. For it is the natural impulse of all created beings to recognize God and know that all their strength lies with him. When he languished, their very nature made them languish with him. And so the ones who were his friends suffered pain for love.

Recognizing Christ

But it was not only the ones who knew him that felt the pain of his dying. Every being everywhere suffered, because the comfort of all creation was faltering, although the secret power of his protection never failed them.

There were two individuals who did not recognize Christ at first, and they represent the two kinds of people: one was Pilate, and the other was Dionysius the Areopagite. Dionysius was a pagan at the time. When he witnessed the wonders and marvels, the sorrows and terrors that occurred during Christ's dying, he said, "Either the world is coming to an end right now, or else the One who is the Creator of nature is suffering." And so he carved these words upon an altar: *This is the altar of the Unknown God.*

God, in his goodness, creates the planets and the elements to function according to their nature, on behalf of both the blessed and the fallen. But during his dying, that goodness was withdrawn from them both. That is why even those who did not know him experienced sorrow at that time. So was our Beloved afflicted for us, and so do we all stand in suffering with him, and shall stand with him always, until we enter his bliss.

CHAPTER 19

Looking Beyond the Son

I wanted to look away from the cross at that point but did not dare. I was well aware that as long as I gazed on the crucifix I was safe and secure. I had this feeling that if I turned my attention away from the cross, I would be in danger from demons. I saw no reason to expose myself to those horrors. Then a voice popped into my mind, as if coming from a friend, and it said, *Look beyond the Son to his Father.*

I knew I had to either look up or answer. My faith led me to believe that there was nothing between the cross and heaven that could distress me. With all the strength of my soul, I answered inwardly, *No, I cannot look away, for you are my heaven.* I said this because I really did not want to look up. I would rather have been in pain till Doomsday than get to heaven by any other means than through him. I was certain that he who held me so close would release me when he wished.

And so I chose Jesus. Although at this time I only saw him in pain, I did not wish for any other heaven than him, who shall be my bliss when I get there. It has been a comfort to me ever since that I made this choice, in spite of the terrible suffering and sorrow I witnessed at that time. It taught me that I should always choose Jesus, in well and in woe, as my heaven.

Our Inner and Outer Parts

Even though, like a wretch, I briefly regretted having asked for the experience of bearing witness to his agony, I became aware that the part of me that resisted such suffering belonged to the natural weakness and negativity of the flesh, but that my soul did not agree with this, and God certainly did not blame me for it. Regret and conscious choice are two opposites, which I experienced at the same time; one is the outward part and the other the inward. The outer part is our mortal flesh, which will always experience pain and sorrow in this life. Remember, I was suffering greatly from my illness during this time, and this is the part of me that was rebelling. The inner part is in a beautiful, exalted state. It is totally at peace there, deeply in love. I experienced this part secretly. It is from this place that I passionately, wisely, and willingly embraced Jesus.

That's when I realized that the inward part is the master of the outward. The interior neither takes orders from nor pays any attention to the exterior. Its entire focus is on oneing with our beloved Jesus. It was revealed to me that the outward does not convince the inward of its position but rather, by grace, the inner draws the outer to itself, and both are one-ed in unending bliss through the power of Christ.

CHAPTER 20

He Suffered for Us

I watched our beloved Jesus languishing for a long time. The one-ing between himself and the Godhead gave him the power to suffer beyond all human endurance. I don't only mean that his anguish surpassed that of any other human being, but that no human being from the beginning of time until the last day could possibly measure, describe, or even conceive of the magnitude of his pain. Ponder the contrast between the worthiness of the most exalted, honorable king and his shameful, spiteful, painful death. He who was highest and most worthy was most drastically brought low and utterly despised.

The most important thing to contemplate here is that the one who experienced this passion is God incarnate. Now consider two other things: that he suffered and whom he suffered for.

This showing revealed the exalted nobility of the glorious Godhead and its oneness with the precious tenderness of the blessed body. It also showed the essential reluctance in our human nature to endure pain. As pure and as vulnerable as he was, he was equally strong and powerful in the face of such devastating pain.

And he suffered for the sake of every human being. He saw every individual's sorrow, desolation, and anguish, and, from the depths of his kindness and love, he grieved for us all. The grief his own mother experienced as she witnessed the suffering of her son brought him the deepest sorrow of all. His sweet humanity was so exalted that his grief surpassed any pain imaginable. As long as he was able to suffer, he suffered for us. And now he has risen and is no longer able to suffer, yet still he continues to grieve with us.

As I gazed upon all this, by his grace, I saw that his love for us is so strong that he willingly chose his passion and suffered it humbly, with deep joy and satisfaction. Any soul touched by grace who sees things in this way will truly realize that the pain of Christ's passion exceeds all other pain. And yet all our pain will be transformed into boundless, everlasting joy by the power of this same passion.

CHAPTER 21

Stay with Him

I watched with all my might for the moment when Christ's life would slip away at last. I expected to see his body quite dead, but it did not happen. Then, just when I thought his life could not last a minute longer, and that this showing was about to reveal his final end, everything shifted. As I gazed upon that same crucifix, his facial expression suddenly changed to joy. The transformation of his blessed countenance transformed mine. I became as glad and as merry as I could be.

And then our Beloved cheerfully suggested to my mind, *Is there any point to your pain or your grief, now?* And I found that I was completely happy.

I realized that what Christ meant to show me is that we are hanging on the cross with him right now—in our pain, in our suffering, even in our dying—and that if we willingly stay with him there, he will, by his grace, convert all our distress into delight. He will suddenly change his appearance, and we will find ourselves with him in paradise. No time will elapse between the sorrowful state and the state of bliss. Everything will be reconciled in joy. This is what he meant when he asked me what the point was of my pain and grief now.

And so shall we be fully blessed.

Our Fragile Human Hearts

Then I realized that if he were to show us his most blissful countenance now, no pain on earth (or any other place) could possibly trouble us. We would experience everything as joy and bliss. But because he showed us an expression of the suffering he endured in this life, our fragile human nature causes our hearts to be troubled and demands that we labor with him on the cross.

Do not forget, however, that the reason he suffers is because, in his goodness, he wishes to bring us into his joy. In exchange for the bit of pain we endure in our lives, we will receive a transcendent, boundless knowledge of God, which we could never have without that portion of tribulation. The more intensely we suffer with him on his cross, the greater will be our glory when we are with him in his kingdom.

CHAPTER 22

The Bliss of the Father

Then our beloved Jesus Christ asked me, "Are you well satisfied that I suffered for you?"

And I said, "Yes, good Lord, thanks be to you. Oh yes, good Lord, blessed may you be!"

Then our kind, sweet Lord said, "If you are satisfied, I am satisfied. It is a source of endless joy, bliss, and delight to me that I suffered my passion for you. If I could suffer more, I would suffer more."

At that point, my consciousness was transported to paradise, where I perceived three states of bliss, which astonished me. I thought, *I see three heavens, but they are all part of the blessed humanity of Christ. None is greater than another, or less, neither higher nor lower, but they are all equal in their supreme joy.*

In the first state of bliss, Christ showed me his Father. I did not see his physical form, but I knew who it was from the quality of the encounter and from his actions. That is, through Christ, I recognized the Father. What I mean by action is that God blesses his son, Jesus Christ. This blessing, this gift, is so precious to Christ that nothing his Father could have given him would have brought him greater joy.

We Are His Crown

So this first state, in which the Father honors the sacred offering of his Son, appeared to me as a heaven in itself. It overflowed with bliss. For the Father is well pleased with all that Christ has done for our liberation. We are his, not only by virtue of his setting us free with his passion, but also through the generosity of his Father, who has given us to him. We are his bliss! We are his reward! We are his honor! We are his crown—not his garland of thorns, but his royal circlet. That's the part that amazed and delighted me most: that we are his crown.

What I am trying to say is that we bring Christ such great bliss that he counts all his hard labor, painful passion, and cruel and shameful death as nothing. When he said to me, "If I could suffer more, I would," I realized that he would die as often as he could, and his love would never let him rest until he had done it. I pondered this diligently, trying to figure out how often he would die if he could. The number far surpassed my understanding! My wits could not grasp such vastness. My reason could not take it in. My intelligence did not have that power.

No matter how often he died, still he would consider it nothing in the light of love. He sees everything as nothing compared to his love. Even though his sweet humanity could only suffer and die once, the goodness in him can never cease from offering itself. He is prepared to do the same every single day, if only it were possible. If he said he would create new heavens and new earths for love of me, it would not move me nearly as much. He could create new heavens and new earths every day if he wanted to, but to die for my love so many times that it exceeds the greatest number imaginable? This, in my opinion, is the most exalted offer our beloved Lord could make for the human soul.

So, what he means is, *How would it be possible for me not to do all that I could do for love of you? This deed does not disturb me, since I would, for love of you, die and die again, and suffer and suffer again, paying absolutely no attention to my pain.*

Love Is Greater Than Pain

This brings me to the other way we can contemplate his blessed passion. The love that made him suffer his passion is greater than all his pain. His love is as far beyond his pain as heaven is from earth. For the pain was part of a noble, honorable act, done once, and compelled by love. This love is without beginning, and shall be without end. It is because of this love that he uttered these sweet words, "If I could suffer more, I would suffer more." He did not say, "If it were absolutely necessary, I would suffer more." Because even if it weren't necessary, he would do this over and over again for our love.

God ordained this deed and action for the benefit of our liberation as perfectly as God could ordain it. Here I saw that Christ's bliss was complete. His bliss would not have been complete if things could have been any better done than they were done.

CHAPTER 23

Within this triple phrase, "It is a source of endless joy, bliss, and delight to me," God revealed to me three more states of bliss. Joy stood for the Father's pleasure; bliss for the Son's honor; and delight for the Holy Spirit. The Father is pleased; the Son is honored; and the Holy Spirit is happy forevermore.

The Joy That Permeates the Passion

With this I received a new way of contemplating his blessed passion. I saw the joy that permeates his passion and makes him take delight in it. All the aspects of his passion that I had witnessed led to this final phase. Our gracious Lord first showed me his bleeding head, next the discoloration of his face, then the deep slashes in his body from the scourging and the copious blood that flowed from them, followed by the profound drying of all the moisture in his flesh, and finally the joy and bliss of the passion.

God wants us to rejoice with him in our liberation. He wants us to take deep comfort in this and be strengthened by it. With his grace, he wants our souls to be completely and joyfully engaged. For we are his bliss, and he delights in us and wishes for us to delight in him, with his grace. All that he does for us, and has done, and ever shall do, does not cost him a thing and has never been a burden to him, nor ever will be. He paid one fixed price during that time, which began with his sweet incarnation and lasted until his blessed rising on Easter morning. With the completion of this deed, the debt was paid, we are liberated, and Christ endlessly rejoices.

The Cheerful Giver

Sweet Jesus, let us pay attention to the delight the blessed Trinity takes in our liberation! Let us be equally delighted! Let us strive, with his grace, to find as much joy in our liberation as Christ has, for as long as we are here on earth!

The entire Trinity was at work in Christ's passion, blessing us, through him, with an abundance of virtues and plentiful grace. Only the maiden's Son suffered, while the whole of the Trinity rejoices forever. This was highlighted for me when he said, "Are you well satisfied?" and then when he said, "If you are satisfied, I am satisfied." It was as if he had said, *Your satisfaction is enough to give me everlasting joy and delight. I ask nothing more than this in exchange for my service.*

He reminds me of the cheerful giver, who pays little attention to the thing he is giving and instead focuses all his desire and intention on pleasing and soothing the one to whom he is giving it. If the receiver accepts the gift gladly and graciously, then the courteous giver counts all his cost and labor as nothing compared to the joy and delight he derives from bringing pleasure and comfort to someone he loves. This was generously and fully revealed to me.

Contemplate the magnitude of this word, "ever." For this word opens to an exalted awareness of God's love for our liberation and the multitude of joys that arise from the passion of

CHAPTER 24

Gazing into His Side

Then, with a cheerful expression, our Beloved looked into his side and gazed into his wound with joy. With his sweet gazing he directed the mind of this creature to enter through that wound in his side. There he revealed to me a beautiful and delicious place, ample enough for all humanity to rest in peace and love. This made me think of his dear blood and the precious water that he allowed to be poured out for love.

Then he showed me his sacred heart, cloven in two. With sweet rejoicing, he partially revealed to me the nature of the Godhead, strengthening my poor soul to be able to understand what I saw: the endless love that is without beginning, always is, and evermore shall be.

And with this revelation, our sweet Lord said, with passionate bliss, "Oh, how I have loved you!" It was as if he had said, *My darling, behold and see the Lord, your God, who is your Creator and your endless joy. See your own Brother, your Savior. My child, behold and see the utter delight and bliss I take in your liberation. For love of me, enjoy it with me now.*

Oh, How I Have Loved You

To deepen my understanding, he said these blessed words, "See how I have loved you!" It was as if he had said, Behold and see that even before I died for you I loved you so much that I wanted to die for you! And now I have died for you and have willingly suffered what I could. Now all my bitter pain and cruel labor have been transformed into endless joy and bliss for me and for you. How could there be any blessing you could pray for that I would not joyously grant you? Your pleasure is my pleasure. Your endless delight in me brings me unending delight.

This is the meaning, as simply as I can express it, of these blessed words, "Oh, how I have loved you!" Our Beloved revealed them to make us all exceedingly happy.

CHAPTER 25

Would You Like to See Her?

With the same expression of mirth, our good Lord looked down on his right side, toward where Our Lady stood during the time of his passion. "Would you like to see her?" he asked me. With these sweet words it was as if he had said, *I know you, and you wish to see my blessed mother! For, after myself, she is the greatest gift that I could reveal to you and the greatest joy and honor to me. All my blessed creatures long to see her.*

Because of the extraordinary, exalted, wondrous love Christ has for this sweet maiden, his blessed mother, Our Lady Saint Mary, he revealed her in all her joy. It was as if he had said, *Do you want to see how much I love her, so that you can rejoice in the love I have for her and she has for me?*

These sweet words of our good Lord are meant for all humanity, as if he were addressing all of us as one person, saying, *Do you want to see in her how deeply I love you? For love of you, I have made her so noble, so worthy, so sublime. This delights me, and I wish to delight you.* After himself, Mary is the most blessed thing he could possibly reveal to us.

This showing did not make me yearn to see her physical form. Rather, I wanted to see the virtues of her blessed soul—her truth, her wisdom, her love—and from this come to know myself better and increase my loving awe of God.

Radiant Mother

After our good Lord had shown me his blessed mother and said these words, "Do you wish to see her?" I answered, "Yes, beloved one, thank you! Yes, sweet Lord, if it is your will, yes!" I had often prayed to encounter the maiden, and I expected to see her physical form, but this is not the way Jesus revealed her to me. Instead, with those words he spoke he gave me a spiritual vision of her. Where before I had perceived her as so little and simple, now I saw her in all her glory—radiant, regal—more pleasing to him than all created beings. And so he wants all who rejoice in him to rejoice in her, to share the delight he takes in her and that she takes in him.

For a greater understanding of this, he showed me this example: When a person loves another creature with all his heart, above all others, he would like to make all creatures love and delight in that creature whom he loves so much. And so when Jesus said, "Do you want to see her?" it seems to me these were the most delicious words he could utter to accompany the spiritual vision of his mother he revealed to me. For the Beloved never did show me any specific person other than Our Lady Saint Mary, and he showed her to me three times. The first time was when she conceived, the second was in her time of sorrow beneath the cross, and the third was as she is now: radiating honor and joy.

CHAPTER 26

It Is I

After this our Beloved revealed himself to me in a much more glorified form than I had ever seen. He showed me that our soul will never find rest until it comes into him and understands that he is the fullness of all joy. He is simple and gracious, the source of true life and unending bliss.

Our beloved Jesus often said to me:

It is I,

It is I;

It is I who am most exalted;

It is I whom you love;

It is I who delights you;

It is I whom you serve;

I am the one you long for.

I am the one you desire.

I am the object of your intention.

I am all.

It is I whom Holy Church preaches and teaches you about.

It is I who has showed myself to you here.

The sheer number of the words he spoke surpasses my wit and reason. It is such a vast number that it transcends all my abilities to calculate or convey. I think that is because these words speak of that which surpasses all the heart can wish or the soul can desire. And so because I cannot say what these words mean, or comprehend it myself, it is up to each of you, with the grace of God, to interpret them as God intended: with love.

PART II

EVERY KIND OF THING SHALL BE WELL

CHAPTER 27

All Will Be Well

Our Beloved reminded me of the longing I had for him before, and I realized that nothing stood in my way except sin, which is the thing that stands in everyone's way. It seemed to me that if there were no such thing as sin, we would all be as pure as our Lord created us, reflecting his likeness. And so, like a fool, I used to wonder about this. Why wouldn't God, in his omniscience, have prevented sin when he created us? If he had left sin out of creation, it seemed to me, all would be well. I know I should have abandoned this disturbing line of thought, but I couldn't seem to help myself. I grieved and lamented this beyond all reason and discretion.

But in this showing Jesus gave me all that I needed. "Sin is inevitable," he said, "yet all will be well and all will be well and every kind of thing shall be well."

I Saw No Sin

In this naked word, "sin," my Beloved brought to my mind a general sense of all that is not good. I saw that this was connected to the shameful contempt and dreadful tribulation he endured for us in this life, and in his dying, and in the spiritual and physical suffering of all created beings. For we are all troubled to some degree, and we shall continue to be troubled as we follow our Master Jesus to the place where we are fully purified. Eventually we will be stripped of our worldly flesh, and all the inner inclinations that are less than good will fall away.

As I beheld this, I understood that the passion of Christ encompasses all the pain that ever was or ever shall be, and that his was the worst pain of all—even greater than the greatest pain. I saw all this suffering in a fleeting glance, which quickly turned into comfort. For our beloved Lord does not want to terrorize us with this ugly sight.

But the truth is, I did not see any sin. I believe that sin has no substance, not a particle of being, and cannot be detected at all except by the pain it causes. It is only the pain that has substance, for a while, and it serves to purify us and make us know ourselves and ask for mercy. The passion of our Lord gives us comfort against all this. That is his blessed will. The tender love that our Beloved has for us moves him to console us swiftly and sweetly.

What this means is, *It is true that sin causes all this pain, but all will be well, and all will be well, and every kind of thing shall be well.*

Not an Iota of Blame

When he said these gentle words, he showed me that he does not have one iota of blame for me, or for any other person. So, wouldn't it be unkind of me to blame God for my transgressions, since he does not blame me?

At the heart of these words I saw a wondrous, exalted secret hidden in God, which he will openly reveal to us in paradise. With this secret knowledge we will finally understand why he allowed the suffering of sin to come into this world, and we will endlessly rejoice.

CHAPTER 28

Shattering Compassion

When I saw the compassion our Beloved has for our transgressions, my own heart was filled with compassion for all my fellow spiritual seekers. In the same way that I was filled with pain and compassion for the passion of Christ, now my heart overflowed on behalf of God's servants, whom he so deeply loves. Just as a person shakes a cloth in the wind, Holy Church will be shaken in sorrow, anguish, and tribulation in this world.

But our Lord revealed this to me: "I shall turn this into a great thing—a thing of endless honor and everlasting joy." I saw that our Beloved rejoices (with sympathy and compassion) in the hardships his servants endure, and he lays on everyone something humiliating, which he does not consider a flaw, but which makes the world scorn and despise them, abuse them and cast them out. He does this to protect them from the harm that would come if they were too prideful and arrogant. They need to distance themselves from the petty pretensions of this wretched life and allow the Beloved to prepare them for paradise, where he will exalt them in his everlasting bliss.

I heard him say, *I shall utterly shatter you. I will empty you of your vain inclinations and bitter pride. After that I will gather*

you up and infuse you with humility and gentleness. I will make
you pure and holy. I shall one you to myself.

We Do Not Suffer Alone

Then I saw that every impulse of loving compassion we have toward our fellow human beings is the Christ in us, and every kind of humiliation he suffered in his passion is revealed in our compassion. There are two ways to look at what our Beloved means. The first is the bliss he brings us into, and in which he wants us to rejoice. The other is comfort in our pain. He wants us to know that all our pain will be transformed into blessings and honor by virtue of his passion. He wants us to realize that we never suffer alone, but always together with him, and to rest in him as our foundation. And he wants us to see that his pains and his tribulation so far exceed our greatest suffering that no one can fully grasp it.

If we carefully contemplate his intention for us, it will keep us from grumbling and despairing in the face of our pain and grief. Although we may think we deserve to suffer because of our sins, we need to believe that his love excuses us. Our courteous Beloved dismisses all blame. He looks upon us with nothing but sympathy and mercy, as the children we are: guileless, innocent.

CHAPTER 29

Repairing the Sin of Adam

As I sat in contemplation of this showing, reflecting broadly, sorrowfully, and darkly on its meaning, I felt an upwelling of fear and exclaimed to our Beloved, "Oh, good Lord, how can all be well? The transgressions of your creatures have caused such harm!" As much as I dared, I wished for a fuller explanation of this matter, so I could put my mind at ease.

My Beloved responded gently and with the most loving expression. He showed me that the most harm that has ever been done, or ever will be until the world ends, was caused by Adam. The entire Holy Church proclaims this. He wanted me to acknowledge his glorious reparation and realize that this is infinitely more pleasing to the beloved Godhead than Adam's sin was harmful. This is what our blessed Lord means. He wants us to pay attention to this teaching: *Since I have set right the greatest of transgressions, I want you to rest assured that I will make well everything that is less serious.*

CHAPTER 30

Room for All

He revealed two aspects of truth in this showing.

The first part is that our Savior and our salvation are open and clear, beautiful and luminous and ample. There is room enough for all of humanity here. We are bound to this part by God and powerfully attracted to it. The same grace by which the Holy Spirit teaches us inwardly Holy Church outwardly instructs us in. This is the truth our Beloved wants us to engage with, rejoicing in him as he rejoices in us. The more abundantly we accept the grace from this, with reverence and humility, the more bountiful the blessing we receive from it and the more fully we earn his gratitude.

Secret Teaching

The second part is hidden. The Beloved's secret teaching is sealed from us. It is appropriate for God to hold his secret counsel in peace. It is appropriate for his servants, out of reverence and respect, to let go of our desire to understand his mysteries. Some of us are so busy trying to uncover his secrets! He has compassion for people like this. But if only we knew how much it would please him and relieve ourselves of our burdens to abandon that desire, we would immediately let go.

Do the saints in heaven wish to know anything other than what God chooses to reveal to them? No! They surrender to his will in all matters. Do they make themselves love him? They do not. Their devotion is the natural outflow of his will. We should be like the saints and want what they want. We should desire nothing other than God's will for us. In God's will, we are all one.

In this way I learned that we should rejoice in our blessed savior Jesus and place all our trust in him.

CHAPTER 31

I Have the Power to Make All Things Well

There was not a single question or doubt I raised for which our good Lord did not have a reassuring response. "I have the power to make all things well," he said, "I know how to make all things well, and I wish to make all things well." Then he said, "I shall make all things well. You will see for yourself: every kind of thing shall be well."

By saying, "I have the power," he is referring to his authority as the Father. "I know how" coincides with the wisdom of the Son. Saying "I wish" points to the volition of the Holy Spirit. The entire blessed Trinity is unified when he says, "I shall." And where he says, "You will see for yourself," I believe he is including the whole of humanity.

With these five phrases, God wishes us to be enfolded in peace and rest. In this way, Christ's spiritual thirst will be alleviated at last. His thirst is our thirst, and our thirst is our love-longing, which will endure until the day of judgment, when we will be together at last. Those of us who will be one-ed with Christ, bringing him endless joy and bliss, are still here in this world, and more of us are being born every day. This is his thirst. This is his love-longing. He yearns to gather us all into himself, bringing us endless joy and bliss. We are not wholly inside him now, but we will be.

Human and Divine

Our faith teaches us (and these revelations confirm) that Christ is both God and human. Regarding the Godhead, he is our supreme bliss, and has been since the beginning of time and shall be until the end. This boundless joy, by its very nature, cannot be increased or decreased. This was beautifully revealed when he said, "It is I who am most exalted."

Regarding Christ's humanity, our faith teaches us (and these revelations confirm) that, with the power of the Godhead and for the sake of love, he endured unspeakable suffering—his passion and his dying—to bring us into his bliss. These are the offerings of Christ's humanity, and he rejoices in them. He assured us of this when he said, "It is a source of endless joy, bliss, and delight to me that I suffered my passion for you." This is the sublime beauty of Christ's actions. This is what he meant when he said, "You are my bliss; my reward, my honor, and my crown."

And Christ is our crown, also. He is our head! In his glorified form, he transcends all suffering. In his humanity, into which all human beings are woven, he is not yet fully glorified and is not beyond suffering. He still feels that burning thirst he felt on the cross. As I see it, Christ's thirst—his desire and his longing—has been with him always, and always will be, until the last soul is liberated and is lifted into his bliss.

Longing

As truly as God embodies the quality of compassion and mercy, so does he embody the quality of thirst and longing. The power of this longing in Christ awakens the longing in us. Indeed, we cannot come to paradise without this holy yearning. The quality of thirst and longing, just as much as the quality of mercy, is rooted in the boundless goodness of God. These are two different things. As long as we are in need, Christ will continue to experience the very essence of spiritual thirst, and the energy of his longing draws us to himself. And so he has mercy on us, and he yearns for us, but his wisdom and his love do not allow him to put an end to this longing until the perfect time.

CHAPTER 32

You Will See for Yourself

Once our Beloved said, "Every kind of thing shall be well," and on another occasion he said, "You will see for yourself: every kind of thing shall be well." My soul recognized a number of teachings contained in these phrases.

This was one: He does not only pay attention to lofty and noble things, but also to things that are humble and small. He cares about the one as much as the other, this as well as that. When he says, "You will see for yourself: every kind of thing shall be well," he is referring to this level of care. He wants us to know that he will not forget the least little thing.

Here is another: From our point of view, there are many actions in this world that seem to be done with evil intent, and we see that they cause great harm. It seems impossible to us that such things could ever have a good outcome. When we think about this, our hearts are filled with such sorrow and grief that we cannot rest in joyfully beholding our God, which we would like to do. The problem lies with our faulty reason. We are too blind to comprehend the wondrous wisdom of God, too limited to grasp the power and goodness of the blessed Trinity. That's why he says, "You will see for yourself: every kind of thing shall be well." It's as if he had said, "Hold this in your heart, in faith and trust, and everything will be revealed to you in the end, and you will see it all in the fullness of joy."

Hidden Blessing

And so I draw deep comfort from these words, "I have the power to make all things well," and I know that our Beloved has many great blessings in store for us. There is something else that the blessed Trinity will do on the last day. I don't know what it is or how it will be done. No creature lower than Christ will know about it until it happens. The loving goodness of our Lord God wishes for us to be aware that it will be done, yet his power and wisdom, which stem from that same love, choose to hide from us exactly what it will be and how it will be done.

The reason he wants us to know about it at all is that he wishes our souls to rest in ease and our hearts to abide in peaceful love, avoiding the temptation to pay attention to anything that could hinder our true joy in him. Yet it must, for now, remain a secret. It is enough to know that our Beloved intends to bestow a great blessing on us, which he has kept hidden and treasured in his holy breast since before time began. This is the deed, known only to him, that will make all things well. Just as the blessed Trinity created all things from nothing, so the blessed Trinity will make all things well that are not well.

How Could All Be Well?

This insight struck me with awe, and I contemplated the teachings of our faith, trying to make sense of something that was bewildering me. Our faith is grounded in the word of God, and it directs us to believe that God's word will always be preserved.

78

One of the things our faith says is that many creatures will be damned. Like the angels whose pride caused them to fall out of heaven and become demons, there are those on earth who die outside the faith of Holy Church and are said to be bound for hell. Some of these creatures are heathens and others are Christians who live unchristian lives. We are taught to believe that they will be isolated from God's love for all eternity.

And so how could it be that every kind of thing shall be well? In light of this teaching, it seems impossible! The only answer I could find in any of my showings was when our Beloved said, "What is impossible for you is not impossible for me. I will keep my word in all things, and I shall make all things well." In this way I learned, by the grace of God, to remain steadfast in the teachings of my faith, but that I should also wholeheartedly believe that every kind of thing shall be well, as our Lord revealed to me in these showings.

This is the great blessing that our Beloved will bestow, and by which he will keep his word and make everything well that is not well. Still, what that deed is and how he will do it remain a mystery to any mind inferior to the mind of Christ. At least that is what I understand from what the Lord revealed to me at this time.

CHAPTER 33

Nothing about Hell

As far as I dared, I wished to be shown a fuller understanding of hell and purgatory. It was never my intention to challenge the teachings of our faith in any way. I am in full agreement with Holy Church about the purpose of hell and purgatory. I simply wanted, for the sake of learning, to comprehend every aspect of our faith's teachings, including this one, which I did not really understand. In this way, I hoped that I could better honor God and improve my life.

Yet, in spite of this desire, I learned nothing whatsoever about hell and purgatory. The only thing that even came close was the showing in which God revealed to me that he completely dismisses the spirit of evil. From this I inferred that any creature who shares the character of the spirit of evil—whether they have been baptized or not—are similarly dismissed when they die. No more mention is made of them in front of God and his holy ones than of the devil. They simply cease to exist. Even though all my showings revealed almost nothing about evil, I was not tempted to contradict any article of faith taught to me by Holy Church.

For instance, while I saw several showings of Christ's passion and felt a glimmer of the suffering Our Lady and his true friends experienced when they saw him in pain, I did not see anything about those who put him to death. My faith teaches that God condemned these people and endlessly damned them (unless they were converted by grace before they died), but not a single thing was revealed to me about this.

God gave me the strength to cleave to the teachings of our faith without exception, holding fast to everything I had believed before these showings. I prayed hard to be in alignment with Holy Church, by the grace and mercy of God, and never stray from this until the day I died.

It is God's will that we honor all his deeds. Through our recognition of all he has done in the past, we will know, trust, and believe in all he shall do in the future. What we need to do is to stop meddling and trying to figure out what his ultimate blessing will be. Instead, we should desire to be like our brothers and sisters who are saints in heaven and wish nothing but that God's will be done. Then we shall rejoice in God alone and be equally satisfied with both his concealing and his revealing. This showing taught me that the more we busy ourselves in uncovering his secrets in this or any other matter, the farther we will be from knowing.

CHAPTER 34

Mystery

Our beloved God revealed to me that there are two kinds of mystery. One is the Great Secret, with all the particular secret details it encompasses. He wants us to understand that these are things that will remain hidden until the time comes when he will clearly reveal them to us. The other kind of mystery is made up of all the secrets he opens to us, such as the secrets he revealed in these showings. He wants us to understand that it his will that we know them.

It is not only God's will that makes some things a mystery to us; it is also because of our blindness and ignorance that we do not understand them. He has profound sympathy for these weaknesses of ours. That's why he sometimes chooses to reveal them to us himself, so that we will know him, and love him, and cleave to him. Our Beloved will fully and graciously reveal to us everything that is to our advantage to know. One of the ways he does this is through the preaching and teaching of Holy Church.

God showed that he is very pleased with all the men and women who firmly embrace and humbly accept the preaching and teaching of Holy Church, because he is one with Holy Church. He is the foundation. He is the essence. He is the teaching and the teacher. He is the goal toward which every loving soul aspires, and he is our reward. Every soul to whom the Holy Spirit declares this knows it or will know it. And I truly hope that he will come to the assistance of all souls who seek in this way, for they are seeking God.

Everything I have said here—and the things I will say later—should offer consolation about sin. For when I saw in a showing that God does all that needs to be done, I did not see any sin, and I saw that all is well. And then when God did reveal something to me about sin, he reassured me that "All will be well."

CHAPTER 35

A Certain Creature

Once the almighty God had revealed his goodness with such abundance and plenitude, I decided to ask another favor: I wanted to know if a certain creature I loved would continue on the good path that, by the grace of God, I believed this creature had begun to walk. But I seem to have hindered myself with this desire. I was not shown a thing about this.

But then an answer came into my mind, as if offered by a friendly intermediary: "Accept this in a general way, and contemplate the grace of our Beloved as he reveals it to you," the voice said. "For it is a far greater honor to God for you to glorify him in everything, everywhere and always, than in any one special thing." I agreed. I realized that if I were to act wisely and follow this teaching, maybe nothing in itself would make me particularly happy, but I would also not become especially anxious or distraught about anything in particular, either. For "All will be well." To behold God in all things is to live in complete joy.

Righteousness and Mercy

By the same blessed power, wisdom, and love with which our Beloved created all things, he is constantly leading all created things to the same glorious outcome. When the time is right, we shall see it. Everything our Lord God does is righteous, and everything he tolerates is honorable. Both good and evil are included in these things. He does all that is good and tolerates all that is evil. It's not the evil itself that is honorable; it is our Lord's tolerance of it that is worthy of honor. Through the action of his mercy and grace, through his wondrous humility and gentleness, we come to know his unending goodness.

Righteousness is something so good that it cannot be better than it is. God himself is true righteousness. All his actions have been rightfully ordained for all eternity by his supreme power, supreme wisdom, and supreme goodness. Just as he ordained everything for the best and continuously works to bring all things to the best end, he is always perfectly pleased with himself and his actions. The soul that, by grace, beholds this blissful harmony is filled with its sweetness. All beings destined to be liberated and eternally dwell in paradise are created righteously in the eyes of God. His endless goodness protects us and wondrously lifts us above all creatures.

Mercy is an action that comes from the goodness of God. As long as sin is allowed to pursue righteous souls, mercy will continue acting through him. When sin no longer has permission to pursue them, there will be no further need for mercy, and that action will cease. That's when everything shall be brought into full righteousness and shall remain that way without end.

Sometimes, with his tolerance, we do miss the mark and fall. In his blessed love and through the power of his wisdom, we are protected. And by mercy and grace we are lifted to ever-greater joy. And so he wishes to be known and loved, in righteousness and mercy, now and forever. The soul that wisely contemplates this and, through grace, holds onto these two things equally shall endlessly rejoice.

CHAPTER 36

The Great Deed

My Beloved showed me that something is going to happen, and that he himself will make it happen. It will be a marvelous thing—honorable and generous—and it will have something to do with me. With this revelation, my heart soared with joy, for I saw that I might go on missing the mark, but this will not hinder him in the slightest from blessing me with his great goodness. Beholding this truth is the highest joy for a soul in awe of God who, more and more and through his grace, naturally desires nothing but that his will be done.

This great deed shall begin right here, with us. It shall honor God and abundantly bless his lovers on earth. It shall endure until we reach paradise, where we will see and understand everything at last, and we will rejoice. And this joy and honor shall radiate throughout heaven, toward God and all his holy ones, forever, without end. This is why God revealed this thing to me: so that I would see it and interpret it, and that we would all rejoice in him and his works.

As this showing continued to unfold, I saw that this great deed was yet to come, that he himself would take care of everything, and that my only task was to accept it wisely, faithfully, trustingly, and with joy. But he kept the nature of this act a secret from me. This made me realize that he does not want us to ever be afraid of what he will do to us. He reveals glimpses of his great deeds because he wishes for us to know about them and, through this knowledge, come to love him and delight in him and endlessly rejoice in him.

Whenever God reveals something like this, of such abundant honor and benefit to us, it is because he loves us so much. Yet, that which remains hidden is also an expression of his great love. This showing is meant to help us recognize and believe that all his secrets will ultimately be opened to us and connect us to his unending bliss. We should equally rejoice in that which he reveals and that which he conceals. If we do this willingly and humbly, we can rest in surrender and find comfort and ease there. And God himself will thank us for it.

Something to Do with Me

When he says that this thing he shall do has something to do with me, I understand that I am simply a representative of all souls. This great deed shall be done for all of us. It shall be honorable and fruitful and marvelous, and God himself shall do it. All we will do is continue missing the mark. It doesn't matter. This amazing truth brings us the highest possible joy.

It is as if our beloved Lord had said, *Behold and see: Here is humility; here is love; here you know yourself; here you rejoice in me. Rejoice in me! Of all the things you can do, this is what pleases me most.*

As long as we are in this life, whenever we foolishly turn our attention to those we deem not to be on a spiritual path, our Lord God tenderly touches us and blessedly calls to us, speaking to our souls: *Let me be the only object of your attention, my beloved child. Focus on me alone, for I am enough for you. Rejoice in your savior and your salvation.*

I am sure this is our Beloved working in us. The soul that is pierced with this truth, by grace, shall see it and feel it. This great deed is meant for all humanity and does not exclude particular souls. I am not given to know what our Beloved wishes to do for each of his poor creatures. Remember the great deed I mentioned before? That is different from the one I'm talking about now. This one begins here and now. The other one will happen when we arrive in paradise. Every person to whom God gives this gift here on earth will know it in his own way. The great deed I spoke about cannot be known either in heaven or on earth until it happens.

Miracles

In addition to this teaching, he gave me a special understanding of miracles. "It is well known that I have performed many miracles in the past," he said. "They were numerous and exalted, astounding and honorable and great. But I have never stopped making miracles, and I never will." Everyone knows that sorrow and anguish, challenges and tribulations, come before miracles. That is so we will recognize our own powerlessness and see that we have fallen into misfortune through our tendency to miss the mark. This knowledge humbles us and deepens our awe of God, causing us to cry out to him for help and grace.

That's when great miracles begin to happen. They come from the exalted power, wisdom, and goodness of God. To the extent that it is possible in this transitory life, these miracles show his strength and reveal the joys of paradise, bolstering our faith and raising our hope in love. And so it pleases God that we know him and honor him through his miracles. That's why he does not want us to become overly disheartened by the sorrows that befall us or the temptations that besiege us. It has always been this way before miracles come.

CHAPTER 37

I Will Keep You Safe

God reminded me that I'm bound to miss the mark. But I was so absorbed in gazing at him that I did not immediately grasp what he was saying to me about this. So our beloved Lord, in his merciful way, simply waited. When I was ready, he gave me the grace to listen. Although this showing was very personal, the comforting teachings that followed helped me to understand that I was supposed to accept these revelations on behalf of all humanity. When he showed me that I would continue missing the mark in my life, he meant that we all would.

As this realization penetrated my mind, I was filled with a gentle anxiety, but my Beloved responded in this way: "I will keep you safe." He said this with such love and steady reassurance, and my spirit felt so protected, that I cannot possibly express it.

Just as I was shown that I am going to miss the mark whether I intend to or not, I saw that God will keep me safe no matter what, and that the same is true for all my spiritual companions. What could make me love my fellow spiritual seekers more than to see that God loves them all as one unified soul? For in the higher part of every individual soul on the spiritual path there is a spark of the Divine will that never has and never shall consent to sin. There is also a savage will in the lower part of humanity that is incapable of willing anything good. But the God-part is so good that it triumphs over the animal-part, and he loves us for who we are and delights in what we do.

In this way, God showed me that we are completely lovable in his sight and we stand fully at the center of his love. He loves us now while we are here, and he shall love us when we come to stand before his blessed face. It is not for lack of God's love that we fall into suffering, but through our own ignorance and lack of love.

CHAPTER 38

Sin Is the Source of Honor

God showed me another thing: sin is a source of honor, rather than shame. While it is true that for every sin there is corresponding pain, we are blessed an equal measure of love. Just as we suffer various pains in this life in accordance with the severity of our various sins, we shall be rewarded in heaven with various joys in proportion to the victories we achieved in suffering the consequences of our negative actions here on earth.

Every soul whom God brings home to himself is so precious to him, and its place at his table one of such great honor, that the goodness of God could never permit them to suffer for the actions they already paid for in their lifetime. Even some very serious sinners are honored by Holy Church here on earth and in heaven for all eternity. This realization lifted my heart to great heights, as God brought several beloved sinners to my mind.

Beloved Sinners

From the Old Law, there were David and many others like him. From the New Law, there were Mary Magdalene, both Peter and Paul, and Thomas of India. Then there are our own John of Beverly and innumerable others who are recognized by the Church along with their sins. There is no shame in this, because all their transgressions have been turned into honor. In this way our Beloved gives a glimpse of what things are like where he dwells. What we see in part here is fully realized there: he transforms all things, no matter how ugly or sorrowful, into blessing.

Our Beloved showed me a familiar figure, in order to comfort me: St. John of Beverly. Here is a very exalted saint, who is also a neighbor close at hand, and we are all acquainted with him. The Lord called him "St. John of Beverly," just as we do, and he said this with a very sweet and cheerful expression, indicating that John is a very high and blessed being in his sight. Then he went on to remind me that when John was a tender youth he was intensely devoted to God. He maintained a deeply loving awe of the Lord, and yet still God allowed John to miss the mark. But he also protected him, so that, even when John fell, he did not lose any progress on his path.

Afterward, God raised him to many times more grace. In proportion to the humility and contrition John exhibited in the way he lived in this world, God gave him joys in the next world that far exceeded anything he would have experienced if he had not missed the mark and fallen. This is reflected in the many miracles that continue to happen around John's body. Our Beloved does all this to lift our spirits and make us happy in love.

CHAPTER 39

A Contrite Heart

Sin is the harshest affliction that can burden our souls. It is a scourge that strikes men and women, and so severely damages us in our own eyes that we judge ourselves as unworthy of anything other than to sink into suffering. But then our wounds begin to heal, and our souls start to revive. The Holy Spirit leads us to unburden our hearts to a spiritual guide and confess our transgressions nakedly and truthfully, with genuine sorrow and humility that we have dishonored our beautiful God. We accept the consequences for our actions and willingly make the amends suggested by our confidant.

We have countless opportunities for humility in this life, and God cherishes them all. We bear illnesses he sends us inside our own bodies. We endure sorrow and shame inflicted from the outside. We accept the contempt and disdain of the world, with all the temptations and grievances it throws at us, both physical and spiritual.

When it seems that he must have totally given up on us and cast us away—and we are convinced that it's our own fault—our Beloved protects us with the greatest care. The humility we gain through our troubles lifts us very high in God's sight. Also, through his mysterious grace, God himself fills us with contrition, compassion, and true yearning for him. These gifts are so powerful that they spring us from our self-made prison of sin and pain, and lift us to bliss so that we become equal with the exalted saints.

By contrition we are washed clean. By compassion we are made ready. By true longing for God we are rendered worthy. These are three paths guaranteed to lead all souls to heaven, regardless of mistakes we may have made here on earth. These are the medicines that heal every soul who has missed the mark.

Glorious Compensation

God sees the healed wounds of the soul as honors, rather than as penalties. In proportion to the pains and penances with which we are afflicted in this life, the courteous love of our almighty God rewards us in the afterlife. He does not want anyone to lose the slightest degree of benefit from his labors here on earth. He does not blame his lovers for their sins; he knows that these things have already caused us great sorrow and suffering.

Our compensation will not be trivial. It will be exalted, glorious, filled with goodness. In this way, all our shame will be transformed into honor and ever-greater joy. Our gracious God does not want us to fall into despair on account of our so frequently and so grievously missing the mark. Our shortcomings do not in any way diminish his love for us.

Peace and love are always living and working within us, but we are not always in peace and love. Our Beloved wants us to realize that his love is the ground of our whole life. He is our everlasting protector, mightily defending us against all our adversaries, who can be so fierce, so cruel. When we miss the mark, we open ourselves to their attack, and that's when we need his protection all the more.

CHAPTER 40

Welcome Home

This is the way our gracious God expresses his supreme friendship: He protects us with exquisite tenderness whenever we miss the mark. And when he touches us, he touches us secretly, revealing our shortcomings by the sweet light of his mercy and grace. Yet once we have seen ourselves besmirched by our transgressions, we imagine our Beloved must be angry with us. This is when the Holy Spirit fills us with the urgent desire to change our lives and guides us to make amends for any harm we have done. Our efforts to appease God bring peace to our soul and softness to our conscience. We hope that God has forgiven us then, and he has.

At that point our gracious God shows himself to us, merry and glad, with a friendly countenance and a cheerful greeting. He welcomes us as if we have been released from a prison where we had been languishing in pain. Sweetly, he says, "Oh my darling, I am so glad you are here! I have always been with you, through all your woe. Now that you see me loving you, we are one in bliss."

And so, by the agency of the Holy Spirit and the virtue of Christ's passion, our sins are forgiven again and again. Through

God's mercy and grace, he welcomes our souls in honor and joy here on earth, just as he will joyfully and honorably receive us in the world to come.

What I truly understood from this showing is that the great goodness of God has made all things possible for us. This is true to such an extent that all we have to do is rest in loving peace within ourselves, and God will keep us fully safe. But because that kind of trust is almost impossible for most of us in this life, we must rely on the power of sweet prayer and love-longing, in partnership with our beloved Jesus. Remember when he gave us a glimpse of extreme spiritual thirst? This is the intensity with which he yearns to complete our joy.

Separation

No man or woman should use the consoling teachings I have just offered as an excuse to say, "In that case, I might as well go ahead and commit transgressions, because I will be rewarded for my bad behavior," or even, "sin is no big deal." Beware of this impulse to minimize the negative effects of missing the mark: such thinking is erroneous and comes from the spirit of evil.

For the same true love that blesses us all with its comforting power also teaches us that we should reject sin for the sake of love alone. My own feelings convince me that the more clearly our souls perceive the gracious love of God, the less likely we will be to miss the mark and the deeper our remorse when we do. In fact, if all the pains of earth, purgatory, and hell were laid in one pile, and sin in another, it would be better to choose all that pain than sin, which is separation from God. There is no crueler hell than to be separated from God. The sin of separation is the only pain a loving soul must reject. Everything other than this is good. Nothing but this is evil.

When we set our intention on love and humility, then, by the power of mercy and grace, we are cleansed and made whole. God's willingness to save us is equal to his power to do so. Christ himself is the foundation for human behavior. He teaches us to return evil with good. He is the embodiment of this love. He does for us what he teaches us to do for one another. He wants us to be like him: wholly loving toward ourselves and toward all beings. He does not want us to withdraw our love from ourselves or from other beings any more than he would ever withdraw his love from us as a result of our missing the mark.

Simply reject sin, and endlessly love the soul, as God loves it. In this way we learn to let go of evil as God lets go of it and embrace the soul as God embraces it. Let God's words bring you endless comfort: "I will keep you safe."

CHAPTER 41

I Am the Ground of Your Prayer

Next, our Lord taught me two things about prayer: one had to do with righteous intent; the other was about absolute trust. We often fail to trust God completely. Either we can't really believe that he hears us or we feel unworthy of reaching out to him, or (worst of all) we feel absolutely nothing, finding ourselves as empty and dry after our prayer as before. And so our own foolishness is the cause of our weakness. Believe me, I know—I have experienced this myself.

Our Beloved brought all this to my mind and showed me these words: "I am the ground of all your praying. First, it is my will that you have what you long for (oneing with me). Next, I am the one who makes you long for it. Finally, I cause you to pray for it. So how could it be that you would not get what you ask for?"

With these three statements our good Lord gave me powerful encouragement. He taught me that true prayer yields great joy and endless benefit. He showed me something impossible: that is, when we pray for mercy and grace, it is impossible not to receive mercy and grace. Everything that our good God causes us to pray for he has already ordained for us since before time began. And so we can see that it is not our praying that makes God give us mercy and grace. Mercy and grace come from God's own goodness. That's what he revealed when he said these sweet words: "I am the ground of all your praying." Our Beloved wants his lovers here on earth to recognize this. The more we recognize this, the more we will be inclined to pray, which is our Lord's intention.

Prayer is the manifestation of the true, gracious, enduring will of the soul, at one and held fast to the will of the Beloved through the secret power of the Holy Spirit. As I see it, our Lord himself is the first one to receive our prayer. He accepts it with profound gratitude, then sends our prayer up above, and places it in a treasure house where it will never die. Our prayer rests there before God, surrounded by all his holy saints. Our prayer is always accepted, always furthering our progress on the path. When we come at last to our ultimate bliss, he shall give our prayer back to us as a gift of gratitude, filled with endless honor and boundless joy.

Pray without Ceasing

Our Beloved is exceedingly glad and happy about our prayer. He watches for it and yearns to receive it, for our prayer, through his grace, makes us like him. It is his blessed will that we be like him, not only in our nature (which we already are and always have been) but also in our will. That is why he says, "Pray inwardly, even if it seems to give you no pleasure. It is bringing great benefit, even if you do not perceive it. Pray inwardly, even if you sense nothing, see nothing, even if you think you are achieving nothing. For it is in dryness and emptiness, in sickness and weakness, that your prayer pleases me most. Don't you see? Your whole life is a prayer in my eyes."

God wishes us to pray without ceasing, and he wants to generously reward us for this. The Beloved accepts the good intentions and dedicated labor of his lovers, no matter how we feel. It pleases him when we work in both prayer and good living, with his help and by his grace, reasonably and with common sense, keeping ourselves strong for him until the day comes when we receive the One we seek in fullness and joy. That is what Christ was referring to when he said, "You shall have me as your reward."

Giving thanks is also part of prayer. Thanksgiving is a true, inner awareness. Charged with the quality of reverence and loving awe, we turn ourselves with all our might toward the actions our good Lord guides us to, rejoicing and thanking him inwardly. Sometimes the soul is so filled with gratitude that it overflows and breaks into song: "Good Lord, thanks be to you! Blessed are you, O God, and blessed may you always be."

And then sometimes when the heart is dry and feels nothing, or maybe is being tempted by the spirit of evil to give up on God, both reason and grace drive the soul to cry out to the Lord, imploring him in a loud voice, recalling his blessed passion and his great goodness. And so the power of our Lord's word enters the soul and enlivens the heart. By his grace, we begin to engage in true practices and pray a blessed prayer and rejoice in our Beloved. This is the holiest prayer—the loving prayer of thanksgiving—in his sight.

CHAPTER 42

He Prays through Us

There are three things our Lord God wants us to understand about prayer. The first is that prayer originates with God himself. This is what he means when he says, "I am the ground of all your praying." When he says, "It is my will that you have what you long for," he means that prayer flows from and returns to his goodness.

The second thing God wants us to know about prayer has to do with the manner in which we practice. Our will needs to be transformed into the divine will, and we need to rejoice in our praying. That's what he means when he says, "I am the one who makes you long for it."

The third thing God wants is for us to understand the fruit that we harvest through prayer: that is, to be one-ed with and made like our Lord in every way. That is the entire purpose of this love-lesson. He wants to help us! All we need to do is to let him pray through us, just as he says. Blessed may he be!

Ample Trust

Here is our Beloved's will: that our prayer and our trust be equally ample. For if we do not trust as deeply as we pray, our honoring of our Beloved is incomplete. Also, we drag ourselves down and cause ourselves pain. I think this comes from the fact that we do not really believe that God is the ground in which our prayer blossoms. We do not recognize that prayer is the gift he gives us through the grace of his love. If we really knew this, we would fully trust that our Beloved will give us all that we desire.

I am certain that no one genuinely asks for mercy and grace unless God has already placed mercy and grace inside him. Yet sometimes it crosses our minds that we have been engaged in prayer for a long, long time and have still not received the object of our heart's desire. This should not make us sad. I truly believe that what is happening is either that a better time is coming for our wish to be granted or more grace is yet to be given—we are meant to wait for an even more marvelous gift. He wants us to know beyond all doubt that he himself is the ground of existence. He wants us to root our understanding in this truth, with all our might, all our intention, and all our purpose. He wants us to take our rightful place on this foundation and dwell here.

Nobly Made

By the light of his own grace, he wants us to understand three things. One is that we have been most excellently and nobly made. Another is that we have been beautifully and lovingly redeemed. Finally, God protects everything he has created in a field of love for our benefit. This is what he means when he says, "Behold! I have done everything you asked before you were even born. And now you exist, and you pray to me." He wants us to realize that the greatest deeds are being done, just as Holy Church promised.

As we contemplate this, we should pray with gratitude for the completion of the divine task that has been set into motion.

We should pray that he guide and direct us for the greatest good in this life. We should pray that he bring us into his bliss and realize that he has already done all that we could ever wish for. God wants us to see that he is the Doer and to pray for him to do. It's not enough to pray to God without recognizing that he is the one who does everything. Without this awareness, we will grow sad and doubtful, which dishonors God. On the other hand, if we have an intellectual understanding that God is the one who does all, but we do not practice prayer, we are not living righteously.

God wants us to balance an active life of prayer with a clear understanding that he is the ground of our praying. In this way, he is honored and we are supported. It is God's will that we pray for all that he has already ordained—either specifically or generally. As I see it, the joy and bliss this gives to God, and the blessings and honor we derive from it, surpass the understanding of every creature in this life.

Joy Is Our Birthright

Prayer is comprised of a right understanding that the fullness of joy is our birthright, along with intense yearning and unshakable trust. When we engage in prayer, the lack of the bliss we were born to experience fills our souls with longing. True understanding and love, driven by sweet recollection of our Savior, give us the grace to trust in God. And so it is according to our nature that we yearn and by his grace that we trust. God is constantly watching for these two functions in us. It is our duty to both yearn and surrender. God expects nothing less of us.

When we rise to this task of prayer through our very best efforts, we are likely to think that our labor is nothing. And we would be right. Still, let us do what we can. All we need is to humbly ask for his mercy and grace. We shall find in him all that we lack in ourselves. This is what he means when he says, "I am the ground of all your praying." In these blessed words, along with the full showing, I perceived that we shall be fully victorious over all our weaknesses and doubting fears.

CHAPTER 43

Partners with God

Prayer unites the soul with God. Even though the inner essence and true nature of the soul are always like God, the effects of our behavior do not always reflect this likeness externally. Prayer becomes the witness that the soul wills as God wills. It soothes the conscience and shapes us for grace. And so it is God who teaches us to pray and trust with all our might that what we long for shall be given. He looks at us through the eyes of love. He wants us to be partners with him in our goodwill and our good deeds. He moves us to pray for that which it pleases him to do. Then he returns the favor of our inner state of prayer and longing—which he himself instills in us—and gives us an external reward.

When God said, "If you ask me, I will give you what you long for," he revealed to me such pleasure and delight, as if he were truly grateful for every good thing we do. And yet he is the one who does it! He loves that we pray so hard to align our will with his. He seems to be saying, "How could you possibly please me more than to pray with all your might—wisely and willingly—to do the thing that I am already going to do?" In this way, through prayer, the soul and God come into perfect accord.

When, through his loving grace, our courteous God reveals himself to our soul, we have all that we desire. For that moment, we do not perceive any lack. All we want to do is fix our attention on him with all our might and totally lose ourselves in contemplation of him. As I see it, this is an exalted, utterly invisible state of prayer. The whole purpose for praying is to be made one with the vision and contemplation of the One we long for. In a true state of prayer, we rejoice, stilled by holy awe, filled with such sweetness and delight in him that, for the moment, we cannot pray at all. We can only go where he moves us in the moment.

The more the soul sees God, the more the soul desires to see God. Our longing comes from his grace. I am well aware of this. But when we do not see God in this way, then we feel a deep need to pray. We sense that we are falling short and are somehow unfit to be with our Beloved. This moves us to reach out to him in prayer. When the soul is tempted, troubled, left to herself in her disquiet, it is time to practice prayer. She needs to ask to be made soft and supple, aligned with the divine will. For the Divine does not align himself to our will. No amount of prayer will makes God conform to us. He is eternally shaped like love.

Seeing God Face-to-Face

What I realized is that whenever we have the urge to pray, our Beloved is following us, intensifying our longing. And when, by his special grace, we plainly gaze upon him, beholding nothing but him, we are following him, and he draws us to him with the power of love. I clearly saw and fully felt that his wondrous and abundant goodness completes us and strengthens all our abilities.

Then I perceived that his continual working in every kind of thing is so beautifully done—so wise and so powerful—that it surpasses our greatest imagination. God's goodness transcends

107

all thought, all comprehension. At that point, all we can do is contemplate him and rejoice. We allow ourselves to be filled with the overwhelming desire for oneing with our Beloved, to listen deeply for his call. We delight in his goodness and revel in his love.

And so, through his sweet grace, in our own humble and unceasing prayer, we will come to him now, in this life. If we are simple enough to bear his many secret touches and sweet spiritual glimpses, he will give us the oneing we desire. It is through the grace of the Holy Spirit that this shall be done. We will long for our Beloved until the day we die. And on that day we will merge with our Beloved, knowing ourselves clearly and possessing God completely. We will be endlessly hidden in God, seeing him truly and touching him fully, spiritually hearing him, deliciously smelling him, and sweetly tasting him.

Ultimately we shall see God face-to-face, and he will be completely familiar when we meet him. Then the created creature shall fully behold God her Creator and eternally contemplate him. No one can see God in this way and survive—not in mortal form. Yet when, in his special grace, he wishes to show himself to us here on earth, he strengthens the creature beyond her own natural power, and he measures out the revelation according to his own will, so that she can handle it and it does her the most good.

CHAPTER 44

Truth Sees, Wisdom Contemplates

In all the showings, God often revealed to me that we human beings continuously perform his will and honor him always, without end. He demonstrated this in the first revelation, when he showed me the marvelous truth and wisdom in the soul of our blessed Lady, Saint Mary. I am hoping, by the grace of the Holy Spirit, that I will be able to put into words what I understood about this.

Truth sees God. Wisdom contemplates God. When these two things come together, a third gift arises: the wondrous delight in God, which is love. Where there is truth and wisdom, there also is love. They flow from the same divine source. God creates all that is, yet is himself uncreated. He is supreme and everlasting truth, supreme and everlasting wisdom, supreme and everlasting love. The human soul is a created thing, which does what it was made to do: see God, contemplate God, and love God.

That is why God rejoices in his creation and creation rejoices in God. They are endlessly marvelous to each other. In the act of marveling, we behold our God—our Beloved, our Maker—

utterly exalted. He seems so good, so great in comparison to us that we creatures perceive ourselves as practically nothing. Yet the clarity and brilliance of truth and wisdom help us to see that we are made for love and that in love God will keep us.

CHAPTER 45

Human Judgment

God judges us according to our true essence, which he keeps, whole and safe, inside himself always. Divine judgment reflects our Beloved's righteousness. But human judgment reflects our changeable fleshliness. Now we are attracted to one thing, now something else, depending on external appearances. Human judgment is muddled. Sometimes it is gentle and kind; other times it is harsh and painful. Kind and gentle judgments reflects the righteousness of God. Our beloved Jesus takes our cruel and oppressive judgments and redeems them, through mercy and grace, through the power of his blessed passion, and so transforms them into righteousness. And so God reconciles and unifies these two opposites, while acknowledging them individually in his eternal consciousness.

God's righteous judgment arises from his exalted and endless love. I saw this sweet and lovely judgment in that beautiful revelation in which he made it clear that he assigns no blame of any kind. Yet even though this showing was delicious and delightful, it did not fully comfort me. I was still concerned about the judgments of Holy Church, which I had learned about in the past, and which I constantly held in my mind. By this Church judgment, it

111

seemed necessary for me to regard myself as a sinner. By this same judgment, I had to acknowledge that sinners sometimes deserve blame and anger. But I could not find blame and anger anywhere in God!

Conflicted

This conflict filled my heart with such intense turmoil that I cannot possibly describe it. God himself showed me the higher judgment, and I was compelled to accept it. At the same time, I could not seem to give up the lower judgment previously taught to me by Holy Church. I longed for God to show me the way in which what Holy Church teaches here on earth is true in his sight. I wanted him to help me to understand it in the best possible way. How could these seemingly opposite judgments come together in such a way that God is glorified and I walk a righteous path?

All I could do was to keep this question in my heart, where it will remain until the day I die. I continued to wish for the ability, by grace, to distinguish between these two judgments in the best way for me, personally. For all heavenly things, and all earthly things that belong to heaven, are contained in these two perspectives: loving-kindness and recrimination. The more we understand these two kinds of judgment, with the gracious guidance of the Holy Spirit, the more we will perceive and know the ways in which we fall short. The more truly we see ourselves, the more naturally, by grace, we will yearn to be filled with the endless joy and bliss for which we have been created. The essence of our human nature is now, has always been, and ever shall be overflowing with God's blessing.

CHAPTER 46

Know Yourself

It is only by faith that we can know the true self here in the fleshliness of this passing life. Once we clearly see and truly know our self, we shall clearly see and truly know our God in the fullness of joy. And so it is bound to be that the closer we come to our ultimate bliss, the more our own nature and God's grace fan the flame of our yearning.

In this life, we can acquire knowledge of ourselves through the assistance and support of our own exalted nature. And, through mercy and grace, we can increase our self-knowledge and continue to grow. But we can never know ourselves completely until the last moment of this passing life, at which point every kind of pain and woe will come to an end. And so, both by nature and grace, we are rightfully endowed with the yearning to know ourselves with all our might. In the fulfillment of this knowledge, we shall come to clearly and truly know our God in the fullness of never-ending joy.

Throughout the entire time of my showings, I observed two things. One was that divine love is boundless and will continue forever, which infused me with an unshakable security in my total protection and blissful salvation. This, in fact, was what the whole revelation was about, from beginning to end. But the other observation had to do with the common teaching of Holy Church, in which I had been previously instructed and grounded. I willingly held to this teaching, both in practice and in thought. This commitment to the teaching of Holy Church never left me in the face of my showings. Rather, the showings taught me to love the teaching and take delight in it, for in this way, and with the help and grace of our Lord, I could rise to an ever more exalted knowledge and more profound loving.

Contrary to His Nature

And so, as I contemplated the showings, it seemed necessary to me to see and understand that we do miss the mark. We do many things that we should stop doing and leave things undone that we ought to do. We deserve some blame and castigation for this. Still, notwithstanding all this, I saw that in truth our Beloved is never angry, nor ever shall be, for he is God. He is good; he is life; he is truth; he is love; he is peace. His power, wisdom, and loving-kindness leave no room for anger.

I clearly saw that it is contrary to the nature of his power, the nature of his wisdom, and the nature of his goodness to be angry. God is himself the goodness that is incapable of anger, for he is nothing but goodness. Our soul is one-ed with him, and he is unchangeable goodness. There can be neither anger nor for-giveness between God and our soul. For the goodness of God has made our soul so completely one with him that there can be absolutely nothing separating us. It was this awareness that led my soul by love, and drew my soul by power, in every single rev-elation. Through his great goodness, our Beloved showed me that this is so and how it is so. He also showed me that he wants us to strive to understand this, insofar as it is in our nature as creatures to understand such things.

It was God's will that everything this simple soul understood be shown and known. For, out of love, he himself powerfully and wisely hides those things he wishes to keep secret. These showings revealed to me that there are many hidden mysteries that cannot be known until God in his goodness has made us worthy of knowing them. I am perfectly satisfied with this. In awe and wonder, I await the unfolding of our Beloved's will. For now, I submit myself to my mother, Holy Church, as a simple child should.

CHAPTER 47

Remission

Two duties belong to our souls. One is to reverently marvel. The other is humbly to endure, always taking pleasure in God. He wants us to remember that life is short and it won't be long until we clearly see, within him, all that we desire. Still, I couldn't help but wonder at the mercy and forgiveness I beheld in God.

Before the showings, I had been taught that the mercy of God was supposed to be manifest in the remission of his wrath when we have sinned. It seemed to me that the wrath of God would be more severe than any other pain to a soul whose intention and desire are simply to love. And so I accepted that remission of his wrath would be one of the main attributes of his mercy. And yet, in spite of anything I saw or wished, I could not see this point in any of my showings. I will attempt, with God's grace, to describe something of what I did see regarding his works of mercy.

We Are Changeable

This is what I understood. Human beings are changeable in this life. We are easily thrown off balance by our frailty, ignorance, and guilelessness, and this causes us to miss the mark. Left to ourselves, we are powerless and unwise. The turmoil of sorrow and woe overwhelms us and conquers our will. It is blindness that causes us to stumble and fall. If we saw God at all times, we wouldn't have any harmful experiences or painful feelings, and we would be free from the distress that accompanies our transgressions.

I felt and saw all this at the same time. Compared to the ordinary range of feelings and perceptions in this life, these things seemed especially exalted and bountiful and gracious. Yet this experience was little and lowly in comparison to the burning yearning of my soul to see God. I saw in myself five movements: rejoicing, grieving, desire, fear, and true hope. I rejoice because God gives me understanding and knowledge, and allows me to see him. I grieve because of my failings. I desire to see him more and more, understanding and knowing that I will never fully rest until I see him clearly and truly in paradise. I was afraid throughout my showings that the vision would fade away and I would be left to myself. And I remain hopeful that, through his boundless love, I will be protected and brought into his bliss.

Rejoicing in his sight, with true hope of his merciful protection, deepens my awareness and gives me great comfort. This mitigates the grief and fear, so that they do not cause me as much pain. And yet I realized that such exalted knowledge of God cannot be sustained in this life. For his own honor and our ever-increasing joy, he sometimes withholds his revelations. We frequently live without seeing him, and we fall back into ourselves, where we cannot find any sense of righteousness. All we can see in those moments is our own inner resistance, which was planted in us when the first human being missed the mark and which we perpetuate through our own willfulness. In this way, a sense of sin and suffering troubles and tempts us in many ways, spiritually and physically, as we make our way through this life the best we can.

CHAPTER 48

Fully Safe

Our sweet Lord the Holy Spirit, who is the endless life that dwells in the soul, keeps us fully safe and makes peace in our soul and gives our soul rest. The Holy Spirit helps us to surrender and reconciles our soul with God. As long as we are walking through this changeable life, this is the way the Beloved is constantly leading us, along the path of mercy.

In my showings, I never saw any anger, except on the part of human beings, and God forgives us for that. For anger is nothing but a stubborn opposition to peace and love. It comes from a lack of power, a lack of wisdom, or a lack of goodness. This lack is not in God, but in us. Our own wretchedness and inclination to miss the mark make us feel frustrated, and we react by shielding ourselves even more fiercely against peace and love. In his constant expression of love and sympathy, our Beloved revealed the truth of this condition to me many times.

The ground of mercy is love, and the flowering of mercy is the way love protects us. God showed this to me in such a way that I could not perceive the quality of mercy as being anything other than rooted in love. As I see it, mercy is the sweet and gracious manifestation of love, mingled with an abundance of compassion. Mercy works in us, protecting us, and mercy works in us, transforming everything into good for us. For the sake of love, mercy allows us to fail sometimes. Inasmuch failing, we fall. And in falling, we die. For in failing to see and feel God, who is our life, something in us perishes. Our failing is frightening, our falling is humiliating, and our dying is tragic. And yet, through all of this, the sweet eye of love and compassion never turns away from us, and the action of mercy never ceases.

Mercy and Grace

I contemplated the quality of mercy, and I contemplated the quality of grace. These are two forms of action in one love. Mercy is the attribute of loving compassion that belongs to the tender Motherhood of God. Grace is the attribute of nobility that belongs to God's royal nature and stems from that same love. Mercy works to protect, sustain, and bring life and healing. It springs from the tenderness of love. Grace works to build up and reward, endlessly transcending whatever we have earned through our loving and labor. It spreads far and wide, displaying the vast generosity and marvelous courtesy of our great God. This all flows from the abundance of love. Grace transforms our shame-filled failings into bountiful and never-ending solace. Grace lifts our terrifying falling into noble, honorable elevation. Grace converts our sorrowful dying into blessed, holy life.

I saw in truth that even as our recalcitrance creates pain, shame, and sorrow for us here on earth, grace, on the contrary, gives us solace, honor, and bliss in the world to come. The grace of God so far exceeds our earthly transgressions that when at last we rise to receive our sweet reward, we will thank and bless our Beloved with all our might, endlessly rejoicing that we ever endured woe. This is the fruit of an attribute of blessed love that

CHAPTER 49

The Opposite of Wrath

During all my showings it was revealed to me again and again that our beloved God cannot forgive, because he cannot be angry. It would be impossible. I observed this with profound wonder and great diligence. Here is what I saw: Our life is grounded and rooted in love. We cannot live without love. And so to the soul who, through his special grace, clearly sees the exalted and wondrous goodness of God, and who knows that we are forever one with him in love, it is the most impossible thing that he could ever be angry. For anger and friendship are opposites.

It is vital for us to believe that the One who dissolves and destroys our wrath and makes us humble and gentle is himself clothed in that same gentle and humble love, which is the opposite of wrath. I saw in truth that wherever our Beloved appears, peace is restored and anger has no place. I did not see any kind of anger in God—neither in passing nor for an extended time. The truth, as I perceive it, is that if he were to be even one iota angry, we would have no life, no place to be, no being. Just as we have our being in the eternal power, wisdom, and goodness of God, so too do we find our refuge in the eternal power, wisdom, and goodness of God. While we may feel anger, disagreement, and strife within ourselves, we are always mercifully enfolded in the Beloved's gentleness, kindness, and humble accessibility.

I clearly saw that our endless friendship, our place in this world, our life, and our being are rooted in God. That same eternal goodness that protects us when we fall, so that we will not perish, continuously draws us to a place of inner peace, which counters our tendency to be angry and argumentative. It helps us to see that we urgently need to seek God and instills a grace-filled desire within us to ask his forgiveness and obtain liberation. We will never be blissfully liberated until we are at peace, and in love, for that is our liberation.

We may still be blind and frail. We may get angry sometimes. We may continue to struggle with the wrath and negativity inside us, which causes tribulation, strife, and woe. And yet the merciful protection of our Beloved keeps us safe and secure, and we do not perish. We will not be wholly and blessedly safe, however, until we all dwell in peace and love. We will not take possession of our birthright of never-ending joy until we find ourselves fully gratified with God and all his actions and judgments, loving and nonviolent toward ourselves and toward all our fellow seekers, and able to love everything God loves. And when we do achieve this state of surrender and love, it is the goodness of God that awakens it in us.

Refuge

In this way I realized that when we are unpeaceful, it is God who is our true peace and our real refuge. He is always working to bring us back to a place of peace inside ourselves. When, through his mercy and grace, we are returned to a state of gentle humility, we find safety. The moment the soul is at peace within itself, it is immediately made one with God, because there is no place in him for wrath. I saw that when we are fully in peace and love, there is no room for opposition or hindrances of any kind. In fact, our Beloved in his goodness transforms any negativity in us and makes it something of value to us.

It is our negativity and oppositional attitude that cause us such suffering. Our Lord Jesus takes these painful things and lifts them up to heaven. They will be made sweeter and more delicious than the heart can conceive or the tongue can tell. When we get there, we will find these things ready for us, fully transformed into radiantly beautiful and exalted honors. And so as the Beloved is our solid foundation here on earth, so he will be our total bliss in the world to come. He will make us as unchangeable as he is.

CHAPTER 50

Seeing as He Sees

The path that leads us ever into grace is made of mercy and forgiveness. According to human judgment, the temptations and sorrows we so often fall into leave us dead. But in the sight of God the soul never died and never will. Still, I marveled at this truth and pondered it with all my might.

"Good Lord," I said, "I see that you are the embodiment of Truth. I know without a doubt that we are guilty of missing the mark all day long. I cannot let go of my belief that we are blameworthy, but I do not see you showing us any kind of blame. How can this be?"

The ordinary teaching of Holy Church, plus my own sense of things, had me convinced that the guilt of our sins hangs on us always, from the original transgression of the First Man to the time when we ascend to heaven. And so it was a miracle to me that I saw the Beloved holding us no more to blame than if we were as pure and holy as the angels in paradise. The contradiction between these two propositions had me utterly befuddled. I was afraid that my vision of his blessed presence would pass before I understood the matter, and I could have no rest until he dispelled my anxiety. I needed to either see that God has dispensed with sin altogether or else the reality of sin as God sees it. If I could see as he sees, then I would know how to view the matter myself, and it could guide my behavior.

The Courage to Ask

The more I gazed upon him, the more intense my longing grew. And yet I had no patience. I was perplexed and afraid. So I turned the question over to God. "What if I concluded that there is no such thing as sin and we are not to be blamed for our transgressions?" I asked him. "Wouldn't that make me blind to truth and more likely to miss the mark? On the other hand, if it turned out to be the case that we are sinners and therefore blameworthy, good Lord, how can it be that I cannot see a trace of this truth in you, who are my God, my maker, in whom I yearn to behold all truth?"

There are three reasons why I felt brave enough to ask him about this. One is that it is not a big thing. If it were some exalted affair, I would be terrified. Another reason is that it is an ordinary matter. If it were some special, secret teaching, I would never have the courage to broach the subject. Finally, if I am going to live here on earth, it seems to me necessary for me to know it. After all, Holy Church teaches that if we have knowledge of good and evil, then, by reason and grace, we can sort the evil from the good, embracing goodness and shunning evil.

I cried out inside myself with all my might, beseeching my Beloved for help. "Ah, Lord Jesus!" I sobbed. "King of bliss! How shall I find comfort? Who will tell me and teach me what I need to know, if I cannot see it in you at this time?"

PART III

YOU WILL NOT
BE OVERCOME

CHAPTER 51

Master and Servant

Our gracious Lord answered by showing me a mysterious and wonderful example of a master and a servant. I saw both beings in physical form. Although this was a bodily vision, my Beloved used it to give me spiritual understanding.

The master sits in dignified repose. He is at peace. The servant sits near his lord, reverent, ready to do his will. The master gazes sweetly at his servant, with love and humility. Then the master sends the servant to a certain place to do something for him. The servant is so eager to do the will of his beloved lord that he leaps up and rushes off to take care of his task. He is in such a hurry that he trips and falls into a deep pit, badly injuring himself. He lies there moaning and writhing. He wails and he groans. But he is incapable of standing up and climbing out of the hole. He cannot help himself in any way.

I saw that the greatest misfortune in all of this was that the servant could find no comfort. He could not turn his head to look back at his loving master, who was nearby and who could have fully reassured him. But for the moment he was feeble and bewildered. So focused on his suffering, all he could see was pain.

And so he waited in terrible distress. In this state of affliction, the servant endured seven great pains.

The first was the severe bruising he sustained when he fell. The second was an unbearable heaviness in his limbs. The third was a generalized weakness, resulting from the combination of these two things. The fourth was that his mind was so stunned and his reason so confused that he almost forgot how much he loved to do the will of his master. The fifth was that he could not get up by himself. The sixth was the pain that most astounded me: he lay there utterly alone. I looked all around and searched the horizons, but I did not see any help for him either far or near, high or low. The seventh was that the place where he lay was deep, constricted, and very hard.

Submitting to Suffering

I was amazed by the way the servant humbly submitted to all this suffering. I watched very carefully to see if I could discern if any of this might be his fault or if the master would blame him for his part in this calamity. I could not detect a single thing the man did wrong. It was only his goodwill and his desire to be of service to his beloved master that caused him to fall. He remained as willing and as good-natured in spirit while trapped in the deep pit as he was when he stood before his lord, ready to do his will.

All this time, his loving master gazed on him with two aspects: one outward, the other inward. Outwardly, the master witnessed the pain of his servant humbly and gently, with great tenderness and compassion. The inward aspect was spiritual, directing my attention more to the lord than to his suffering servant. I saw the master rejoice in the full and noble restoration that he would bring to his beloved servant through his bountiful grace. Then my awareness shifted back to the servant, then back

130

again to the master, until I was able to hold both aspects clearly in my consciousness.

This is when the courteous master began to explain what he meant by all this. "Behold," he said. "Behold my beloved servant. See what damage and distress he has endured in my service, for love of me, yes, and by his own goodwill. Isn't it reasonable that I should reward him for his fear and dread, his injuries and suffering? Not only that, but isn't it my responsibility to give him a gift that far surpasses what the goodness of his former health and well-being would have been? I would be ungracious otherwise."

As the inner, spiritual significance of this revelation began to sink into my soul, helping me see that the suffering was appropriate and even necessary, I realized that it is through the master's goodness and affection that his beloved servant, whom he adored, would be truly blessed and rewarded forever. In fact, the honor he would receive would far exceed what he would have been given if he had not fallen in the first place. Yes, the blessing the lord would give him would be so powerful that it would transform all his wounds and his woe into the highest honor and boundless joy.

Pay Attention to the Details

At this point, the showing vanished, and our beloved God led me straight to the conclusion of the revelation. Although I had to move beyond the details, the wonder of this vision never left me. It felt to me that God had given me the example of the master and his servant in response to my desire for understanding. Yet I could not perceive it clearly enough or interpret it fully enough at that time to provide me any real sense of solace.

I'm going to say that the servant symbolizes Adam, though I saw many different attributes that could not be limited to any individual being. And so because I was not given total under-standing in that moment, I rested in a cloud of ignorance. In many ways, the secrets hidden in this showing remain hidden even now. Still, I realized that every revelation is full of secrets, and so I relied on three insights to guide my understanding.

The first marks the beginning of the full teaching, which I glimpsed even as it was unfolding. The second is the deeper, inner teaching, which I have come to understand over time. The third is the fullness of the entire vision, which our beloved God, in his goodness, continues to bring freely and often to my mind's eye. These three insights are so deeply entwined that I do not know how to separate them. I don't even think it's possible. This three-in-one teaching reminds me to deepen my belief and trust in our Lord God that he shall, by the same goodness and for the same purpose with which he showed me this vision in the first place, interpret it for us when it is his will to do so.

Twenty years after this showing, I received the following inner teaching: *Pay attention to all the attributes and conditions, human and divine, revealed in this example, even if they seem obscure or uninteresting to you.* I willingly agreed to this and set my inner sight on reviewing all the aspects and details that were revealed to me long ago. To the extent that my intelligence and under-standing allowed, I began to ponder the master and his servant, examining the way in which the master sat and the place where he was seated, the color and style of his clothing, his outward appearance, and his inward nobility and goodness. Then I gazed at the servant, at the way he stood and the place he was standing, the color and kind of clothes he wore and how they were made, his outward behavior, and his inner goodness and willingness.

God and Adam

I saw that the master who sat there in such peace and stillness was God, and that the servant represented the first human being, Adam. In other words, God showed me a single fallen human being to illustrate how he looks upon all human beings who miss the mark. In God's sight, all humanity is one person, and all people are a single humanity.

This man was badly injured, his strength diminished. His mind was so stunned from his fall that he turned away from the gaze of his lord. And yet his will remained steady in God's sight. What I saw was that our Beloved praises and rewards human beings for our will to be with him, even when we ourselves are blocked from knowing this. These moments of blindness cause us great sorrow and cruel anguish. At those times, neither can we see our loving Lord, who is so gentle and tender with us, nor do we perceive how utterly that Lord loves us. I clearly understood that if only we could accept the wisdom of these two truths, we would know ourselves and know God. By his bountiful grace, this knowledge would grant us deep peace and true rest here on earth, and the fullness of bliss in the world to come.

This was the first teaching I received from my vision of the master and the servant at that time. I came to realize how God views our tendency to miss the mark. I realized that it is our own pain that blames and punishes us. Our gracious Lord offers nothing but comfort and succor. He is always kindly inclined toward us, loving us unconditionally and wanting only to bring us joy.

Countenance of the King

The spot our Lord was sitting on was simple, situated on the naked earth, a solitary place in the wilderness. His robes were long and flowing, a beautiful blue in color, dignified and befitting a great being. His face was a warm brown, with fine features, his eyes a deep black, radiating loving-kindness. His countenance was merciful. He held within him a sublime sanctuary, high and wide, as spacious as the vast heavens. He continually watched his beloved servant, especially when he fell, and it seemed to me that his loving gaze could melt any heart for love and cleave it in two with happiness. This beautiful expression was a wonder to behold. It was a mixture of compassion and joy, a melding of sympathy and bliss. The joy and bliss surpassed the compassion and sympathy as far as heaven is from earth. For sympathy is a worldly attribute. Bliss is divine.

The Father's expression of mercy and compassion is for Adam, his most beloved creature. His joy and bliss are for his beloved son, who is equal to him. The radiance of his beautiful face filled the whole of the earth, following Adam into the depths of hell, rescuing him from eternal death. This is the mercy and compassion that abide with all beings until the end of time. But humanity is blinded by this life, and we cannot see God as he is. And so when he, of his goodness, wishes to show himself to us, he may appear as a humble man. Still, I understood that we are in no way to equate the divine with the human.

Sitting on Bare Earth

This is what it means that he was sitting on the bare earth: God created the human soul as his throne and his dwelling place. Of all his creation, we please him the most. When we fall into sorrow and suffering, we leave no space for God. We are not prepared to offer such a noble placement. And so our kind Beloved, wishing no other dwelling place than our own souls, sits on the ground and waits, since human nature is mixed with earth. The time will come when God's beloved son will, through his own harsh labor and God's abundant grace, restore the Father to his rightful place of beauty.

The blueness of his robes symbolizes his steadfastness. His beautiful brown skin and dark eyes perfectly reflect his holy dignity. The flowing garments, ample and luminous, symbolize that he has enclosed within himself the breadth of the heavens, all joy and bliss unending. When he directed my attention to himself, I understood all this in a flash. I saw him rejoice in the way he wants to (and shall) fully restore his servant, by his boundless grace. And yet, as I contemplated the master and the servant, I still had questions. So I looked deeper.

Unadorned

The master sat solemnly, the servant standing reverently beside him. There was a double significance to the servant, part inner and part outer. Outwardly, he was dressed as a humble laborer accustomed to hard work. He stood very close to the master—not right in front of him but slightly to the left side. He wore a thin white tunic, old and dirty, stained with sweat, so short that it almost reached his knee, completely unadorned. It was so worn out that it looked like it was on the verge of being ripped to shreds like a rag. As I looked at this, I thought, *How strange! This is hardly appropriate clothing for the beloved servant of a great master.*

But inwardly the servant rested on a foundation of love for his lord that equaled the love his lord had for him. The wisdom of the servant revealed to him an inner understanding that there was one thing he could do that would honor his master. And so the man, compelled by love, completely disregarding his own well-being and not taking into consideration any possible danger, quickly leapt up and ran off to do his master's will. By his garment, I saw that he had been a laborer for most of his life and had only recently been appointed to serve the master. The insight I had indicated that he had never before been sent on such a mission.

Treasure in the Earth

There was a treasure in the earth that the master loved. I pondered what it might be. This is the answer that came into my mind: it is a special food that is completely delicious to him. Remember, I perceived the lord as a man and was amazed that there did not seem to be any food or drink available to serve him. I was also astonished that this great master had only one attendant, and he sent this servant away. I watched closely, eager to see what the servant's task might be.

Then I understood that the servant was about to engage in the most difficult work a person can do: the labor of a gardener. He would be digging ditches, straining and sweating, turning over the soil, reaching deep into the earth, watering each of the plants at the proper time. He would keep working until he had made sweet streams of water flow through the garden and abundant fruits spring from the orchard, and he could carry the harvest home to his master. He would not return home until he had prepared everything perfectly and could honorably present his master with the foods and drinks that delighted him most. And all during this time the master would sit in exactly the same place and wait for the servant he had sent out.

I couldn't help but wonder where the servant came from. I saw that the master has within him endless life and every kind of goodness, but that he wanted only one thing: the earth's treasure, which lay buried inside him in a place of astonishing depth and boundless love. And yet this treasure would not be worthy of the lord until the servant had labored to cultivate and harvest it, bringing it to him and presenting it with his own hands. Other than the presence of the master, there was nothing in that place but wilderness. I did not fully understand the significance of this example. I still wanted to know the servant's origins.

God's Son

The servant reflects the Second Person of the Trinity, and also Adam, which is all human beings. And so when I say "the Son," I mean the Godhead, which is equal to the Father. And when I say "the servant," I mean Christ's humanity, which is the true Adam. The closeness of the servant to the master represents the Son, and his position to the left of the master represents Adam. The master is the Father, God. The servant is the Son, Christ Jesus. The Holy Spirit is the love that is equally present in them both.

When Adam fell, God's Son fell. The true oneing between the divine and the human, forged in paradise, made it impossible to separate them. Adam fell from life into death—into the valley of this miserable world—and descended from there to the under-world. God's son fell with Adam into the valley of the womb of the maiden, who was the most beloved daughter of Adam. By doing this, he redeemed Adam, exempting him from guilt both on earth and in heaven. With tremendous power, he lifted Adam from the depths of hell.

The wisdom and goodness of the servant represent God's Son. The worn clothing of the laborer and his position near the master's left side represent the humanity of Adam, with all the wounding and weakness that attend the human condition. Through this example, God shows us that his own Son and Adam are one and the same. Our strength and goodness come from Christ. Our weakness and blindness come from Adam. Both of these aspects are represented in the example of the servant.

Our sweet Jesus has taken upon himself all guilt. And so the Father can no more blame us than he can condemn his own Son, beloved Christ. He was the servant before he ever came to earth. He stood beside the Father, ready to serve. He waited with determination for the time when God would send him to do that honorable deed that would return humanity to a state of grace. Even though he is God, equal in divinity to the Father, yet he had the foresight and the commitment to become a human being to save all human beings. In this way, he fulfilled his Father's will.

The Leap

And so the Son stands before the Father as a servant, willing to take on our entire burden. He leaps up, totally prepared to carry out his Father's desire. And in the arc of his leap he falls into the maiden's womb, with no regard for his own well-being, overlooking his own suffering. The white tunic represents his tender flesh. Its thinness means that there is nothing separating divinity from humanity. The tight fit represents poverty, and the age of the fabric reflects that it is Adam who has been wearing it. The sweat stains stand for Adam's harsh labor, and the short length indicates the status of a servant.

When I saw the Son standing beside the Father like that, I understood him to be saying, *See, beloved Abba, I stand here in Adam's garment, ready to jump up and run. All I want is to glorify you on earth, whenever you are ready to send me. How long must I wait?* Of course, from the perspective of the Godhead, the Son knew perfectly well when the Father would decide to send him and how long he would be waiting. After all, Christ is the Wisdom of God.

Liberated by Longing

This is what I understood about Christ's human aspect: Christ himself embodies all humanity. His sweet incarnation and blessed passion will liberate us all, because he is our head and we are all the parts of his body. We cannot know the day and time when every sorrow shall pass and all our suffering come to an end. The entire host of heaven longs to know when we will be delivered into everlasting joy and bliss!

It is by our longing that we will be liberated. Through our yearning for oneing, we shall come to be one. The servant standing before his master (or the Son standing before the Father, dressed in Adam's tunic) reflects this deep desire. Christ represents the spiritual yearning in us all. Christ is all spiritual seekers, and all spiritual seekers are Christ. This holy longing springs from God's love and is balanced by humility, submission, and patience, which are also divine virtues he has endowed us with.

As if it were at the beginning of the ABCs, I received essential teachings from this example of the master and the servant. All revelations are full of mysteries, and this one is no exception. Nevertheless, I saw within myself the secrets our beloved Lord had hidden there. I came to understand that the Father sitting at rest symbolizes his divinity. In the Godhead there can be no struggle, only peace. Revealing himself as the master shows our humanity. The servant standing in readiness means labor and service. His position to the left signifies that he is not yet prepared to stand directly in front of God. His rushing off is divine; the action of running is human. The divinity leapt from the Father into the womb of the maiden, descending into form to take on our human nature, and in this descent he was mortally wounded. His wounds are our own flesh, in which he was to experience unbearable anguish and fatal suffering.

Hard Labor

When the servant stood slightly aside, it meant that he felt his clothing was not respectable enough to be in the full presence of the master. As long as he was a laborer, he would not and could not stand directly before the master. Also, he could not rest at the master's side until he had earned this peace through hard labor and selfless service. The left-hand position indicates that the Father aspect of the Godhead willingly released the aspect of the Son to pour itself into form and suffer all the pains associated with the human condition, and not spare him from any suffering.

The servant's torn tunic, on the verge of turning into rags, symbolizes the whips and wounds of Christ's scourging, the thorns and the nails, the tearing of his tender flesh. His writhing and wallowing in the ditch, his moaning and groaning, means that, from the moment he fell into the maiden's womb until he was killed and lay dead, Christ could not supernaturally rise from the conditions of misery. At that point, he yielded the whole of his soul back into his Father's hands, and in doing so delivered all humanity, for whose sake he had been sent.

This was the moment when he first began to reveal his power. He descended into the underworld and pulled up the great root from its depths, which had been rightfully united to him in the highest levels of heaven. His body lay in its tomb until Easter morning. After that day, he would never lie down again. At this point, all the writhing and wallowing, the moaning and groaning, ended. Our damaged mortal flesh was made whole again. Our Savior turned Adam's old tunic—tight, threadbare, and short—into a gleaming garment—fresh and beautiful, white and bright. He was clothed anew in everlasting purity, more ample and luxurious, even richer and lovelier than the clothing I saw the Father wearing! The Father's robes were blue. Christ's clothes were made of light, which blended into a mixture so marvelous that I cannot begin to describe it, for it is composed of pure glory.

Taking Their Rightful Place

Our beloved Lord no longer sits on the ground in the wilderness. Now he sits on the most noble and exquisite seat, which he carved for himself in paradise, and in which he takes great delight. The Son no longer stands before the Father in awe, as a servant stands in trepidation before his master, part naked, dressed only in rags. Now he faces the Father, sumptuously clothed in joyous bounty, a precious crown encircling his head. Remember, an earlier showing revealed we are his crown, representing the Father's joy, the Son's honor, and the Holy Spirit's pleasure, as well as a source of wondrous bliss to all who dwell in paradise.

Now the Son no longer stands to the Father's left in the position of the servant, but is seated at his Father's right hand, in deep rest and boundless peace. Yet this does not mean that the Son sits beside the Father in the same way that two human beings sit side by side. There is no such orientation within the Trinity. Christ sits at his Father's right side, elevated to the highest nobility, infused with the Father's greatest joy. Now the spouse, God's Son, dwells in peace with his beloved wife, the Holy Church, the beautiful bride of endless joy. Now the Son, true God and true human being, rests serenely in the place that the Father so lovingly prepared for him. And the Father is in the Son, and the Holy Spirit is in the Father and in the Son.

CHAPTER 52

Father, Mother, Lover

God rejoices that he is our Father. God rejoices that he is our Mother. God rejoices that he is our Beloved and we are his true lover. Christ rejoices that he is our Brother. Jesus rejoices that he is our Savior. These are five supreme joys and he wants us to rejoice in them, too, and praise him, thanking and loving and endlessly blessing him.

During our lives here on earth, we experience a wondrous mixture of well and woe. We hold inside us both the glory of the Risen Christ and the misery of the Fallen Adam. Christ protects us in our dying and, through his gracious touch, uplifts us and reassures us that all will be well. Adam's fall has broken us all. We are so fragmented, afflicted in our feelings in so many ways, that we hardly know where to turn for comfort. The various pains and transgressions of this life fill our hearts with sorrow and cloud the eyes of our souls.

But we cultivate our intention and wait for God. We have faith in his mercy and grace, and trust that he is working within us. In his goodness, he opens the eyes of our understanding and gives us insight. Sometimes we glimpse more, sometimes we see less, depending on what God gives us the ability to receive. Now he elevates us; now he allows us to come tumbling down.

Sorrowing and Rejoicing

The mixture of sorrow and joy is so powerful that we cannot figure out how to handle it all, let alone assess how our fellow spiritual seekers are doing. The diversity of feelings can be overwhelming. And yet, in those moments when we sense the presence of God, we surrender to him, truly willing to be with him, with all our heart, with all our soul, and with all our strength. This holy assent is all that matters. It eclipses all the wicked inclinations inside us—physical and spiritual—that might lead us to miss the mark.

Sometimes, however, that sacred sweetness lies deeply buried, and we fall again into blindness, which leads to all kinds of sorrow and tribulation. So we must take comfort in the essential article of our faith that teaches us not to give in to our negative impulses, but to draw strength from Christ, who is our defender against all harm. We need to stand up against evil, even if to do so causes discomfort—even pain—and pray for the time when God will once again reveal himself and fill our hearts with the sweetness of his presence. And so we remain in this muddle all the days of our lives. But our Beloved wants us to trust that he is always with us.

God is with us in three ways. He is with us in paradise, True Being-in-Himself, drawing us ever upward by virtue of the spiritual thirst I spoke of earlier. He is with us here on earth, guiding our steps, as I saw when he revealed himself as a single point. And he dwells eternally with us inside our own souls, directing and protecting us.

Cleave to God

Remember: God showed the servant as an example of the blindness and injury involved in Adam's falling and also the wisdom and goodness of God's Son. He showed the master as an example of the sublime nobility and boundless honor that is our birthright through the passion and death of his beloved child. This is why God rejoices so greatly in Adam's fall. The exaltation and bliss that we are given far exceeds what we ever could have had if Adam had not fallen in the first place. And so, at the moment I saw the servant stumble into the ditch, my consciousness was led back to God.

Our sins are the reason for Christ's suffering, and this should cause us to grieve. Everlasting love also caused him to suffer, so for that we should rejoice. Therefore, the creature that sees and senses the operation of love through grace hates only one thing: sin. Of all the opposites on heaven and earth, love and hate are the most irreconcilable. And yet I also saw that our Beloved has arranged things in this life in such a way that we cannot keep ourselves from missing the mark here on earth with the purity and perfection with which we will in the world to come.

Holy Church teaches us that it is by grace that we keep ourselves away from the grave imperfections that would lead us to endless suffering, and we avoid the minor ones through our own common sense and willpower. Whenever our blindness and misery cause us to stumble and fall, we can easily get back up again, energized by the sweet touch of grace. All we have to do is follow the teaching of Holy Church regarding the degree of our sin and move on in love with God. We should not become excessively despondent and give in to despair when we do miss the mark, nor should we be careless and reckless. Rather, let us humbly acknowledge our weakness, recognizing that we wouldn't be able to remain upright for the twinkling of an eye if it weren't for grace and cleave reverently to God, trusting in him alone.

Our Lower Nature

God has one point of view, and human beings have another. Our task is to humbly hold ourselves accountable for our actions, while God, in his infinite goodness, continuously and ever-graciously forgives us. This was reflected in the double-attitude the master showed toward his beloved servant's accident. The first aspect was shown outwardly, with great sympathy and tender compassion, the other inwardly, with endless love. Our beloved God wants us to gently accuse ourselves, clearly perceiving and genuinely recognizing our faults and the harm that comes from them, setting our intention to repair the damage and not repeat it, while at the same time acknowledging the everlasting love he has for us and taking refuge in his boundless mercy. This is all he asks of us, and he himself helps us to do it.

The lower part of human nature was reflected in the master's outward expression, which I saw in two aspects: one was our pitiful stumbling; the other the gracious amends he has made for us. The higher side of human nature was revealed inwardly: it had only a single aspect and was more exalted. For the life and power of the lower side of our nature are derived from the higher, which flows down to us from our own true essence, which is love, through grace. There is absolutely nothing separating the one aspect of the self from the other, for it is all one love.

This blessed love manifests in two ways. In our lower part, we experience it as pain and suffering, compassion and sympathy, mercy and forgiveness, and other beneficial things. In our higher part there is nothing but undifferentiated love and wondrous joy, in which all pain is utterly dissolved. In this showing, our Beloved reveals that not only does he excuse us, but he will also elevate us to a place of great dignity, transforming all our imperfections into boundless honor.

CHAPTER 53

Adam's Fall

I saw that God wants us to know that he does not take the falling of any creature harder than he took the fall of Adam. We know that God loved Adam beyond measure and kept him safe in his time of need, restoring him and raising him to the heights of joy. For our beloved God is so good, so gentle and courteous, that he can never banish anyone forever. And so we praise him forever.

These gracious showings went a long way toward fulfilling my thirst for understanding and easing my terrible fear. I saw and understood that there is a divine will within every soul that would never give in to sin. This will is so good that it could never have evil intent. Rather, its impulse to do good has no limits, and so the soul remains ever-good in the eyes of God. The Beloved wants us to find this truth in the teachings of our faith, namely that we all have this blessed will whole and safe within us. This is because the part of human nature that fills paradise is so completely entwined with Christ's nature that our true essence can never be separated from his, nor should it be. This is a gift of his goodwill and endless foresight.

In spite of this rightful melding and eternal oneing, it is still necessary and beneficial to redeem humanity and pay off our debts. This is what Holy Church teaches us.

No Beginning, No End

I saw that God never started to love humanity, for just as we will ultimately enter into everlasting bliss, fulfilling God's own joy, his love for us has no beginning and he will love us without end. This eternal love is a reflection of his divine foresight and righteous intention. And so with the complete assent of the Trinity, the Middle Person chose to be the ground and head of this beautiful human nature out of which we all arise, within which we are all enfolded, and to which we shall all return. We find our full paradise and everlasting joy in him, sealed by the whole of the blessed Trinity, forever and ever. Before he ever made us, he loved us, and once he made us, we loved him. This love originates in the essential goodness of the Holy Spirit, strengthened by the power of the Father and made wise as a reminder of the wisdom of the Son. In this way the human soul is made by God and oned to God.

I understand that the human soul is created out of nothing; that is to say, it is not created out of any created thing. Instead, it is created from nothing in this way: When God set out to make us, he took the mud of the earth, which consisted of a mixture of materials gathered from all physical things, and formed our bodies. But when he made our souls, he used no materials at all. And so human nature was created rightfully one-ed with the Creator, who is Essential Nature, Uncreated, that is, God. This is why there is absolutely nothing separating the Divine Soul from the Human Soul.

In endless love we are held and made whole. In endless love we are led and protected and will never be lost. God wants us

147

to know that the soul is a life unto itself, one that will endure without end, praising and blessing and loving him in paradise. And just as our existence has no limits, so too are we boundlessly cherished in God, a hidden treasure, whom he sees and knows and loves without beginning or end.

He wants us to know that, while the blessed soul of Christ is the fullest substance and highest possible virtue, the human soul is the noblest being he has ever created. He also wants us to be aware that he knit the beloved soul of humanity into his own when he made us. The knot that connects us to him is subtle and powerful and endlessly holy. And he also wants us to realize that all souls are interconnected, united by this oneness, and made holy in this holiness.

CHAPTER 54

One Love

God's love for humanity is so vast that he makes no distinction between the blessed Christ and the least soul among us. It is very easy to believe and trust that the blessed soul of Christ dwells in the highest realms of the Divine. Yet, if I understand correctly what our Lord means, wherever the blessed soul of Christ is, there too is the essence of all souls.

We would be right to rejoice that God dwells within our own souls, and even more so that our souls dwell in God. Our soul was created to be God's dwelling place, and he who is uncreated is also the place where we dwell. It is a sublime realization to see with inner eyes that God, our Creator, dwells inside us, and it is an even more exalted thing to understand inwardly that the essence of our soul, which is created, dwells in God. It is by this essence that, through God, we are what we are. I saw no difference between the divine substance and the human substance; it was all God. I was able to accept that our essence is in God, that our essence is a creation of God, and that God is simply God.

The all-powerful truth of the Trinity is the Father, who created us and keeps us within him. The deep wisdom of the Trinity is our Mother, in whom we are all enfolded. The exalted goodness of the Trinity is our beloved Lord: we are held in him and he is held in us. We are enclosed in the Father, we are enclosed in the Son, and we are enclosed in the Holy Spirit. The Father, the Son, and the Holy Spirit are enclosed in us. All Power. All Goodness. All Wisdom. One God. One Love.

Our faith is a power that the Holy Spirit sends through our true essence into our sensual soul. All other virtues come to us through this same faith. Without faith, no human could receive any power. Faith is nothing but right understanding, reinforced by true belief and trust in the depths of our beings, that we are in God and God is in us, even when we cannot see this truth. This power—along with all the other virtues God instills in us—does great work inside us. Christ acts mercifully within us, and the power and generosity of the Holy Spirit reconciles us to him. This is what makes us all children of a loving God.

CHAPTER 55

Sensuality

Christ is our way, leading us safely in his laws. With his own body he powerfully lifts us into paradise. I saw that Christ keeps us all with him and graciously presents us to his Father in paradise. Thankfully, his Father receives this gift most courteously—and then gives it back to his Son! This circle of generosity is joy to the Father, bliss to the Son, and delight to the Holy Spirit. Of all the spiritual tasks given to us, this is the one that most pleases our Beloved: that we rejoice in the joy the blessed Trinity takes in the liberation of our souls.

In spite of all our feelings of well and woe, God wants us to understand that our existence is far more real in the realm of spirit than it is on earth. Our faith comes from a combination of the natural love of the soul, the clear light of reason, and the steadfast remembrance of God instilled in us when we were created. From the moment our soul is breathed into our body, turning us into sensual creatures, mercy and grace quickly begin to do their work in us, taking charge of us and guiding us with love and compassion. In this process the Holy Spirit forms our faith and fills us with longing that we will one day merge again with our true spiritual essence, fusing with the power of Christ, enlarged and fulfilled through the Holy Spirit.

I realized that our sensuality is grounded in nature and rooted in mercy and grace, and that this foundation enables us to receive the gifts that lead to eternal life. Our essence is in God, and God is in our sensuality. At the very moment that our soul is made sensual, the dwelling of God is established, divinely placed within us since before the beginning of time. He enters this city and never departs, for God never leaves the soul, dwelling blissfully inside us forever.

Our Higher Nature

God entrusted to his Son all the gifts he could possibly give to creatures, to distribute to us. Christ, dwelling within us, keeps these gifts safely enclosed in himself, until the time comes when we are fully mature in body and soul—our soul integrated with our body and our body with our soul—both assisting and supporting each other as we evolve. Once we have grown to full stature, a process ordained by the essential creativity of nature in harmony with the divine mercy, the Holy Spirit graciously breathes into us the gifts that lead to eternal life.

And so God led my understanding in such a way that I was able to perceive that the soul is a "created trinity," like the uncreated blessed Trinity, known and loved without beginning or end, made one to the Creator by virtue of its creation. This vision was sweet and wondrous to behold, serene and restful, safe and delicious. Because of the glorious unity God forged between the soul and the body, humanity will inevitably be raised from the double death (physical and spiritual). This restoration would not be possible if it had not been for the Second Person of the Holy Trinity who took on the lower part of human nature, which has always been united to the higher part. Both the higher and the lower aspects of human nature, enfolded in Christ, are elements of a single soul. The higher part is one with God, dwelling in the fullness of joy and peace. The lower part takes form and suffers for the liberation of all beings.

I saw and felt both of these parts during that early revelation in which my body overflowed with the memory and experience of Christ's passion and his dying. This showing was accompanied by an ethereal feeling and a secret inner glimpse of the higher part of the soul. I saw this higher aspect at the same time as the lower, and in spite of the suggestion of the intermediary, I could not look up to heaven and away from the suffering of my Beloved, for I was having a simultaneous vision of the inner life. This inner life is the exalted essence, that precious soul, endlessly rejoicing in the Godhead.

CHAPTER 56

Closer Than Our Own Soul

I realized that it is quicker and easier for us to obtain knowledge of God than it is to know our own soul! For our soul is so deeply rooted in God, where it is infinitely treasured, that we cannot come to know it until we have first come to know God, who is the Creator and to whom our soul is one-ed. And yet I also saw that we have within our nature this wise and powerful desire to truly know ourselves. This longing compels us to find our own soul where it is, which is in God. And so, whether we are moved to seek God or our own souls, the Holy Spirit leads us through grace to know them both as one. Both impulses are good and true.

God is closer to us than our own soul. He is the foundation on which our soul stands. He is the energy that keeps the essence and the sensuality together so that they will never separate. In true rest our soul sits in God. In unshakable strength our soul abides in God. In endless love our soul is naturally rooted to God. And so if we yearn to know our soul, to have oneing and dialogue with it, we would be wise to seek our beloved God, in whom our soul is contained. Our essence can be rightly called our soul. Our sensuality, too, can be rightly called our soul. This is because they are one in God.

Our sensuality is the glorious dwelling place in which our beloved Jesus is enclosed, and our natural essence is enclosed within him, while the blessed soul of Christ rests inside the Godhead. I clearly saw that it is necessary for us to experience longing and contrition until we have been led so deeply into God that we truly and completely know ourselves. I also saw that it is our Beloved himself who leads us into this depth, through the same love by which he created us and redeemed us, in mercy and grace. Still, we cannot come to a complete understanding of God unless we come to truly know ourselves. Until our soul has reached its full power, we cannot be fully holy. First our sensuality must be brought up into our essence, through the gifts the Beloved brings us from our tribulations, by his mercy and grace.

Rooted in God

I had a partial touching—a divine inspiration—grounded in nature and reinforced by reason (which is rooted in God, who is the very essence of nature). Mercy and grace spring from God's essential nature and flow into us, penetrating our souls and accomplishing everything needed for the fulfillment of our greatest joy. This is the soil in which our being, our growth, and our fulfillment are planted. It is in our human nature that we have our life and our being. It is in mercy that we have our quickening and in grace our ripening. These are all aspects of a single goodness, and where one operates, all are operating within us.

God wants us to understand these truths, longing with all our heart and all our might to have ever-increasing knowledge of being, mercy, and grace, until such time that our yearning is finally satisfied. To clearly see and fully know these three things are nothing less than the endless joy and bliss we shall have in the life to come, which God would like us to get started on here

CHAPTER 57

We Are Complete

God made us so rich and noble in our essence that all we can do is strive to enact his will and honor him in all things. When I say "we," I mean all true spiritual seekers. I saw how much he loves his lovers, who continuously work to discern what would please him most and never give up trying. As long as our soul is knitted to our body (in the joining of which we become sensual beings), virtues beyond measure flow from this great bounty and exalted nobility.

And so in our essence we are complete, and in our sensuality we are incomplete. God will refill what is lacking and restore us with the action of mercy and grace, which will abundantly pour into us from his own natural goodness. This natural goodness stimulates the flow of mercy and grace, and also the natural goodness that he has given us enables us to receive the action of mercy and grace.

I saw our human nature as being completely inside of God. He creates endless diversity within himself, flowing out of him to accomplish the work of his will, which nature protects, mercy completes, and grace revitalizes. None of this variety is wasted, for the higher part of our human nature is knit to God in creation, and by taking flesh, God is knit to the lower part of our human nature. And so our twofold nature is unified in Christ. The Trinity is encompassed by Christ, in whom our higher aspects are rooted, and he has also taken up the lower part of our human nature, which was assigned to him from the beginning.

Made for Love

I clearly saw that God foresees everything and that all the works that he has ever done or ever shall do have been known to him since before time began. He made humanity for love, and for that same love, he was willing to become a human being himself. If the first good thing we receive from God is our very being, the second is our faith, in which our greatest benefit resides. This is a product of the inflow of the sublimest riches of our higher nature into our sensual soul. Faith is rooted in us and we are rooted in faith through the natural goodness of God by the operation of mercy and grace. And from faith come all the other good things that guide and save us. Among these are God's commandments, which are of two kinds: those we are meant to love and keep, and the things we need to condemn and reject. All our actions belong to one or another of these categories.

The seven sacraments form another element of our faith, which God arranged so that each one follows the one before. Every kind of virtue flows from our faith, for all virtues come from our divine essence, mediated through our humanity, by the goodness of God. In his mercy, God actively renews these virtues through the working of the Holy Spirit. Christ treasures our gifts and virtues within himself. When God knitted Christ's body to ours inside the womb of the maiden, he took on our sensual soul. In taking on our soul, he enclosed us all within himself, knitting our earthly nature to our spiritual essence. In this oneing, he became purely human, for Christ is the perfect human Being, having united all humanity in himself.

Our Lady is our Mother. We are enfolded in her, and from her we are born into Christ. She who is the Mother of our Savior is the Mother of all who shall be saved. And our Savior is our true Mother, in whom we are endlessly born and from whom we shall never be separated.

This showing unfolded with plentiful sweetness and boundless generosity. We are enclosed in him, and he is enclosed in us. He rests in our soul and delights in directing our understanding. He dwells within us in infinite bliss, drawing us ever deeper inward. He wants us to be his helpers in this inner work, giving him all our attention, learning his teachings, keeping his laws, desiring that his will be done in all ways, and trusting him completely. I saw that our true essence is one with God.

CHAPTER 58

All-Power, All-Wisdom, All-Love

Just as God, the blessed Trinity, who is everlasting existence, exists endlessly without beginning, so it was his eternal purpose to create humanity. The original human nature was given to his own Son—the Second Person in the Trinity. When he was ready, in perfect harmony the whole of the Trinity, God created us all at once. He wove us into and united us with himself. In light of this blessed oneing, he keeps us as pure and noble as he created us to be. And through the power of this blessed union, we adore our Creator and delight in him, praising him, thanking him, and endlessly rejoicing in him. The work of this joining is constantly unfolding within every soul.

And so in our coming into being, God All-Power is our natural Father, and God All-Wisdom is our natural Mother, supported by the boundless Love and Goodness of the Holy Spirit. All One God. He is our true partner in this weaving and oneing. We are his beloved spouse, his precious sweetheart, and it is impossible for him to be displeased with us. He says, "I love you and you love me, and our love will never be broken in two."

I contemplated the work of the blessed Trinity, and perceived three aspects: the Fatherhood, the Motherhood, and the Mastery of the One God. Our mighty Father protects the spiritual essence with which he created us and infuses us with bliss. The Second Person—who is our Mother, our Brother, and our Savior—protects our sensuality and liberates and redeems us. Our beloved Lord, the Holy Spirit, offers us compensation and rewards us for all our trouble in this life, exceeding our highest hopes and deepest desires, through his boundless grace and amazing courtesy.

God-the-Mother

Our whole lives are reflected in three aspects. We have our being in the first, our unfolding in the second, and our fulfillment in the third. The first is nature, the second is mercy, and the third is grace. I saw that the exalted Power of the Trinity is our Father, the deep Wisdom of the Trinity is our Mother, and the vast Love of the Trinity is our Master. All of this is contained in our human nature and integrated with our spiritual essence. I realized that the Second Person is really our Mother. This beloved being works with us as a parent here on earth. We were created with a twofold soul, sensual and spiritual. Our spiritual essence is with God-the-Father. Our sensual nature lies with the Second Person of the Trinity, God-the-Mother, in whom we are rooted by virtue of our creation. In taking on our flesh, the Second Person became our Mother of Mercy.

Our Mother keeps all our parts together and works on us in various ways. We profit and grow in Christ-the-Mother. Through her mercy, she restores and redeems us. Through his passion, his dying, and his resurrecting, he makes us one with his own essence. And so the Mother acts with mercy toward all her loving children. Grace, which belongs to the Holy Spirit, joins with mercy, who bestows great gifts on us to reward us for our hard labor and abiding faith. This act of giving is offered freely, with courtesy and grace, surpassing what any creature deserves.

And so we have our being in our Father, Almighty God. We have our restoration and our redeeming in our Mother of Mercy, in whom all our attributes are reconciled and transformed into the perfect human being. And we are completed and made whole through the gifts of grace of the Holy Spirit. Our essence lies in our Father, God-All-Power. Our essence lies in our Mother, God-All-Wisdom. Our essence lies in our Master, the Holy Spirit, God-All-Goodness. Our essence dwells in totality within each Person of the Trinity, which is One God.

Yet our sensual nature is manifested only in the Second Person, Christ Jesus, in whom the Father and the Holy Spirit also live. He energetically lifts us out of hell, delivers us from the misery of earth, and honorably restores us to our rightful place in paradise, blissfully reuniting us with our essence. The power of Christ and the grace of the Holy Spirit combine to increase our spiritual wealth and elevate our nobility.

CHAPTER 59

Source of All Motherhood

It is through mercy and grace that we have all this bliss. And we might never have known such bliss if the quality of God's goodness had not been opposed. Wickedness has been allowed to arise in opposition to that goodness. The goodness of mercy and grace opposed that wickedness and transformed it all into goodness. This is the quality of God that meets evil with good.

And so Christ Jesus, who does good over evil, is our true Mother. He is the source of all motherhood, and we have our being from him, protected by all the sweet love that endlessly accompanies motherhood. As truly as God is our Father, just as truly is God our Mother. She demonstrates this most clearly when she says, "It is I."

What she means is, *I am the Power and Goodness of the Fatherhood. I am the Wisdom and Loving-kindness of the Motherhood. I am the Light and Grace of all blessed Love. I am the Threefold nature of the Divine. I am Unity. I am the supreme goodness in every kind of thing. I am the one who causes you to love. I am the one who causes you to yearn. It is I, the endless fulfillment of all true desire.*

Threefold Foundation

When the soul is lowest, humblest, and gentlest is when it is most exalted and most worthy. All our virtues, all the sensuality given to us as a gift of nature and the assistance of mercy and grace, are built on this essential threefold foundation. We cannot grow without this support. Our exalted Father, God All-Power, is Being-Itself. He knew us and loved us before time began. From this place of wondrous love, with the foresight and unconditional agreement of the blessed Trinity, he willed that the Second Person should become our Mother, our Brother, and our Redeemer. It follows, then, that as truly as God is our Father, so truly is God our Mother. Our Father wills, our Mother works, and our Master, the Holy Spirit, empowers.

Our triple task, then, is to love our God, in whom we have our being, expressing our gratitude with reverence and praising her for creating us, to intensely pray to our Mother for mercy and compassion, and to look to our Master, the Holy Spirit, for guidance and grace. The whole of our life is with these three—nature, mercy, and grace—from which we draw humility, gentleness, patience, empathy, and an aversion to error and wickedness.

And so, by participating in our creation, Jesus is our true Mother in nature. And by taking on our created human nature, he is our Mother in grace. All the loving acts and sweet natural tasks of motherhood belong to the Second Person of the Trinity. From her own great goodness, she endows us with divine will and keeps it safe and whole forever. I saw three ways to look at the Motherhood of God. The first is that she created our human nature. The second is that she took our human nature upon herself, which is where the motherhood of grace begins. And the third is motherhood in action, in which she spreads herself throughout all that is, penetrating everything with grace, extending to the fullest length and breadth, height and depth. All One Love.

CHAPTER 60

Saturating

Now it is time to say a little more about this expanding and saturating action of the Mother, as I understood it. The motherhood of mercy and grace brings us back to our source, where we were created by the motherhood of love. This mother-love never leaves us.

God chose to become our Mother in all ways, humbly and tenderly cultivating the ground of his work in the womb of a maiden. Our transcendent God, the glorious wisdom of the universe, emptied himself into this earthy place and made himself entirely available through our own poor flesh. In this form he himself offered the unconditional service and duties of motherhood. Being nearest to our own nature, the mother's serving is most immediate. Being unconditionally loving, the mother's service is most willing. And being the truest thing there is, the mother's service is most certain. Only God could ever perform such duty.

We are aware that when our mothers give birth to us we end up suffering and dying. But what is this? Our true Mother Jesus, embodiment of all love, gives us a birth that leads only to never-ending joy and eternal life. Oh, what blessing! In love, she labors to carry us inside herself, until we come to full term. Then she suffers the most painful blows and excruciating birth pangs that ever

165

have been or ever shall be endured, only to die in the end. And when she had finished dying, and birthed us into endless bliss, still all this could not satisfy her wondrous love. This is why she said, "If I could suffer more, I would suffer more." He could not die anymore, but he did not want to stop working on our behalf. And so now he must nourish us, which is what a mother does.

Her Tender Breast

The human mother can suckle the child with her milk, but our beloved Mother Jesus can feed us with herself. This is what he does when he tenderly and graciously offers us the blessed sacrament, which is the precious food of true life. In mercy and grace he sustains us with all the sweet sacraments. This is what he meant when he said that he is the one that Holy Church preaches and teaches about. In other words, Christ-the-Mother is entwined with the wholeness of life, which includes all the sacraments, all the virtues of the Word made flesh, all the goodness that Holy Church ordains for our benefit.

The human mother can tenderly lay the child on her breast, but our tender Mother Jesus can lead us directly into her own tender breast through her sweet broken-open side. Here she reveals a glimpse of the Godhead and some of the joys of paradise, with the implicit promise of eternal bliss. This is what he was doing in that showing when he gazed into his side and rejoicing said, "Oh, how I have loved you!"

Beautiful Word

This beautiful word "mother" is so sweet and kind in itself that it cannot be attributed to anyone but God. Only he who is our true Mother and source of all life may rightfully be called by this name. Nature, love, wisdom, and knowledge are all attributes of the Mother, which is God. Even though our earthly birth is low and humble—and so simple compared to our spiritual birth—he is the one responsible for the birth of all babies that are born to their physical mothers.

The kind, loving mother, aware of the needs of her child, protects the child with great tenderness. This is the nature of motherhood. As the child grows in age and stature, she adapts her methods, but her love never changes. And when the child is even older, she allows him to be chastised to counter his vices and develop his virtues and graces. Whenever a human mother nurtures her child with all that is beautiful and good, it is God-the-Mother who is acting through her.

And so, within our human nature, she mothers our lower part through grace, impelled by the love that originates in the higher part. She wants us to know this, so that all our love will flow toward her and cleave us to her. I saw that in truly loving God we pay off all the debts we have to his Fatherhood and Motherhood. This blessed love is a gift from Christ. It is what he was referring to when he said, "It is I whom you love."

CHAPTER 61

Benefits of Falling

The Beloved One cherishes our souls even more than our bodies, and so the tenderness with which God-the-Mother protects us in our spiritual birth is beyond comparison. She awakens our awareness, she opens the way, she eases our conscience, she comforts our soul, she illumines our heart, and she offers us a glimpse of the blessed Godhead. She reminds us of his sweet humanity and blessed passion, infusing us with friendly wonder in light of his exalted, transcendent goodness. She makes us love all that she loves because of her love. She helps us find satisfaction in all God's works. When we fall, her merciful touch lifts us back up, and her loving embrace enfolds us. Once she has strengthened us in this way, her grace inspires us to willingly choose her and offer her our devotion, to be her servant and her lover forevermore.

Once our bond of love has been forged, she allows some of us to experience even more harrowing and painful falls than we did before—or at least it seems that way to us. That's when we start to wonder (because we are not all-wise) if everything we thought about the spiritual life is false, and everything we believed we had accomplished was for nothing. But this is not so. It is necessary for us to fall, and it is necessary for us to recognize it when we do. If we did not fall, we would not realize how vulnerable we are by ourselves, nor how utterly amazing is the love of our Beloved.

When we are delivered to paradise, we will clearly see that we sometimes seriously missed the mark in this life, but that these transgressions never diminished us in her sight nor made her love us any less. Rather, our tribulations and errors in this life are tests, and through them we obtain an exalted and wondrous knowledge of God's love. What a powerful love, that no trespass can break!

This is one way to think about the benefit gained from falling. Another is humility. When we honestly look at our faults, we see that we will ultimately be elevated to the highest heavenly realms, and that we would never be able to achieve these heights if we had not been humbled and laid low. This is why it is necessary for us to witness our own falling, because if we do not see what we have done, we will suffer the negative effects of having failed and not profit from the positive effects of humility. It is through God's mercy that we fall in the first place and take a look at our failing afterward.

The mother may sometimes allow her child to fall and to become distressed in various ways for his own benefit, but her mother-love would never willingly permit any kind of real danger to come to him. Even if our human mothers could not save us from death, our heavenly Mother Christ will never allow us to perish. She is All-Power, All-Wisdom, and All-Love. There is none other like her. Blessed may she be!

Rush into Her Arms

Yet often when our falling and our misery are revealed to us, we become overwhelmed by shame, and all we want to do is run away and hide. Our courteous Mother does not want us to flee.

Nothing would distress her more. She wants us to behave as a child would when he is upset or afraid: rush with all our might into the arms of the Mother. Like a humble child, we say, "My kind Mother, my gracious Mother, my beloved Mother, have mercy on me. I have made myself impure and unlike you. I do not know how to make this right except through your secret help and grace."

Maybe we will not experience immediate relief. We can be sure that this is because she is behaving like a wise mother. If she sees that we would benefit from grieving and weeping, then, out of mother-love, with compassion and sympathy, she will let our suffering run its course until the right time has come for our burden to be lifted. She wants us to be like children, implicitly trusting the love of our mother to protect us in well and in woe.

God would like for us to cultivate our faith through spiritual community and seek our beloved Mother in the solace of true understanding, among the communion of the blessed. For although a single person might often break himself, the whole body of spiritual community can never be broken. And so it is a sure thing—a good and gracious thing—to humbly and powerfully bind ourselves to our Mother, to Holy Church, to Christ.

The flow of mercy, which is his beloved blood and precious water, is enough to cleanse and make us beautiful again. The blessed wound of our Beloved is open, eager to heal us. The sweet and gracious hands of our Mother are already encircling us, diligent and soothing. In everything she does she is like a kindly nurse who has no other task than to attend to the needs of the child. It is her purpose to keep us safe, it is her honor to save us, and it is her desire that we acknowledge this. She wants us to love her sweetly and trust her greatly. This is what Christ meant when he said, "I will always protect you."

CHAPTER 62

Father and Mother of Creation

When she showed all our frailties and failings, our betrayals and denials, our humiliations and burdens and all our woe, they seemed to utterly fill the horizons of this life. Yet along with all this she showed her blessed Power, her blessed Wisdom, and her blessed Love, in which she keeps us safe during these perilous times. When we are suffering, she is holding us as tenderly and guiding us as sweetly for her honor and our salvation as she does when we are experiencing the deepest comfort and ease. She elevates our spirits to the heavenly realms, transforming all our woe into her never-ending honor and our boundless joy. Her love never allows us to waste a single opportunity. It all flows from the natural goodness of God, through the operation of grace.

God is natural in her very being. That is to say, the goodness in nature is God. She is the ground, she is the essence, she is the same thing as nature. And she is the true Father and true Mother of all creation. She caused all of nature to flow out of her to accomplish her will, and all of nature will return to her one day, through the liberation of humanity, in grace. For of all the natures she created, it is in human nature that she placed complete wholeness, power, beauty, goodness, majesty, nobility, reverence, preciousness, and honor.

Universal Truth

Here we can see that we are fully bound to God through our human nature and fully bound to God through grace. Here we can see that we do not need to go far away, seeking various kinds of beings and investigating their natures. We only need to go to our spiritual community, into the Mother's breast, into our own souls, which is where our Beloved dwells. We will find everything we need there—first in faith and insight, afterward within God himself, truly and clearly, in bliss.

But let no man or woman think this truth applies personally to the individual. It does not; it is universal. This beautiful human nature of ours was prepared for our precious Mother Christ. Since before the beginning she recognized, knew, and understood that humanity was created for God's honor and glory, and for the utter joy and bliss of our salvation.

CHAPTER 63

Let Us Not Be Anxious

We can see that it is in our nature to reject evil. Human nature is purely good and beautiful in itself. Grace gives us the strength to turn away from wickedness. Grace annihilates sin and restores human nature to its original, blessed, beautiful source, that is, God. Grace lifts us to an even higher and nobler state than we were in before we missed the mark. For it shall be witnessed by God and all his saints in joy without end that human nature has been tested by the fire of tribulation and that no flaw or lack could be found.

Human nature and grace are in complete harmony. Grace is God, and human nature is also God. He has a twofold way of working, but he is single-pointed in love. Neither grace nor human nature can operate without the other, and they cannot be separated. When, with the mercy and support of the Divine, we reconcile ourselves to both grace and our own nature, we will see beyond all doubt that doing evil is incomparably more wretched and painful than hell, for evil is the exact opposite of the beauty of our true nature. Not only is evil impure, but also unnatural.

It is a terrible thing for a loving soul—who wants nothing more than to be shining and pure for her Beloved, as both grace and her own nature guide her—to detect these faults in herself. But let us not be overly anxious about missing the mark. Instead let us lift our cry to our beloved Mother and ask our Brother Jesus to sprinkle us with his precious blood, making our soul tender and pliant, restoring us to health and wholeness. May this happen gently and in due time, in whatever way is of most glory to him and most joy to us, without end. He shall never cease this sweet and beautiful activity, or even pause, until the Mother has given birth to every single one of her beloved children and set us free.

Childlike Nature

And so our life is grounded in our true Mother, Christ, endlessly guided by his foresight and Wisdom, supported by the boundless Power of the Father, and assisted by the great Goodness of the Holy Spirit. In taking on our humanity, he brought us back to life. In dying on the cross, he birthed us into life everlasting. Ever since that time, and until the Final Days, she nurtures and cares for us, as the supreme loving nature of motherhood mandates and as the natural needs of childhood require.

It is not in the nature of the child to doubt his mother's love, nor is it in a child's nature to rely on himself. It is natural for the child to love the mother and the mother to love the child. Our heavenly Mother is beautiful and sweet in the eyes of the soul. Her grace-filled children are precious and beloved in the eyes of the Mother. She recognizes all the virtues that belong to the nature of a child: our gentleness, our vulnerability, our essential loveliness.

These qualities, and all others like them, are beautiful virtues, which please and serve our beloved Mother. I saw that there is no greater stature in this life than that of a child, who is naturally humble and free from the encumbrances of power and intelligence, until our Divine Mother brings us up to the bliss of our Divine Father. This is what Christ meant when he uttered these sweet words: *All will be well. You will see for yourself: every kind of thing shall be well.* The bliss of our Motherhood in Christ will begin anew in the joy of our Father God, and this new beginning shall be ever renewed, without end. And so I saw that all her beloved children whom she birthed by nature return to her by grace.

CHAPTER 64

I Will Take Away Your Pain

Before these showings, I had an intense yearning to be delivered from this life and from this world. I experienced a constant flow of woe here, in contrast to what I knew to be the well-being and bliss that exist in the world-to-come. Even if there were no pain in this life other than the pain of separation from our Lord, that love-longing sometimes felt like more than I could bear. His absence filled my heart with mourning and yearning. When added to my general misery and weariness, I could find no pleasure in living or in performing my ordinary duties.

My Beloved responded to all this with words of comfort and patience. "Without warning," he said, "I will take away all your pain, all your sickness, your anxiety, and your sorrow. You shall come up to me, and you shall have me as your reward. You will be filled with love, running over with bliss, and you will never again suffer pain or illness, or any other kind of displeasure or lack of inspiration. Instead, you will have joy without end. Why then does it bother you to endure these things for a while, since it is my will and for my glory?"

I realized that God rewards us for surrendering to his will. Since we do not know when our time will come, we must patiently endure until we pass away from this world. It's a good thing that we do not know the time of our death; if we did, we probably would not be able to stand the waiting. Also God has designed it so that as long as the soul is in the body it will feel to us as if we could be taken at any time. For the life we have here on earth, and the languishing that accompanies it, are but a fleeting moment. When God suddenly takes us out of pain and into bliss, it will seem that the pain was nothing at all.

The Bloated Body

At this time, I saw a body lying on the ground. It looked scary and hideous, thick and misshapen, like a bloated heap of stagnant muck. Then suddenly a beautiful creature sprang out of the body. It was a little child, well formed and shapely, quick and lively, whiter than a lily, who nimbly glided up to heaven. The swollen body is a symbol of the misery that often accompanies earthly life. The littleness of the child represents the purity and clarity of the soul.

Interesting, I mused. *There was nothing left of the child's beauty in that bloated body, and not a shred of contamination remained in the child.* It is more blessed, I realized, for a person to be taken from her pain than for pain to be taken from the person. If pain is taken from us, it might come back. And so the inevitability of being taken from our pain is a deep consolation to the yearning soul. In this realization I saw the merciful compassion that our Beloved has for our suffering, embodied in his courteous promise to deliver us. He wants to uplift us in comfort and joy.

It is God's will that we fix the point of our contemplation on the transitory nature of our suffering as often as we can and for as long as we can sustain it, with his grace. This is a blessed contemplation into which God leads our soul, and it is also very much to his glory. And when depression and spiritual blindness cause us to fall back into ourselves, triggered by physical and mental pain, God wants us to know that he has not forgotten us.

Let us take in his promises as deeply and broadly as we can receive them and allow them to comfort us. Let us accept our tribulations as lightly as possible, paying little attention to them, and surrender to waiting. The less seriously we can take our pain, and the less value we place on it for the sake of love, the less suffering it will create for us, and the greater value we will gain from experiencing it.

CHAPTER 65

Holy Awe

I realized that any man or woman who willingly chooses God in this lifetime, for the sake of love, could be certain that he or she is loved with an endless love, which creates grace. He wants us to hold on to this truth and trust in it: we may be as sure of the bliss of divine love here on earth as we will be in the world-to-come. The more delight and joy we take in this certainty, with reverence and humility, the more it pleases our Beloved.

The reverence I speak of is holy awe, which is entwined with humility. The creature sees the Divine as wondrously great and the self as wondrously small. This is a virtue instilled in all God's loved ones. We experience this gift whenever we feel the Presence of God. This holy awe is the experience we most deeply long for, because it creates a wonderful sense of security, true faith, and certain hope. The greatness of love makes this awe sweet and delicious.

Just for Me

It is God's will that I see myself so thoroughly woven to him in love that it appears as if everything he does is done just for me.

This is the way all souls should think about God's love. That is, the love of God creates such a unity in us that no man or woman who understands this can possibly separate himself or herself from any other. And so every soul should see all that God does as being done for him or her alone. He gives us this sense so that we will love him and fear nothing but him. He wants us to know that the power of the Adversary lies in the hand of the Friend.

And so the soul who recognizes this will not be afraid of anything, but instead experience pure awe in the face of the One she loves. All other fears can be dismissed along with the passing maladies of the body and the other passions and fantasies that go along with the human condition. For although we may be in such pain, distress, and sorrow that it seems impossible to think about anything other than what we are experiencing, we pass over it as lightly as we can, as soon as we can, and count it as nothing. Why? Because we understand that it is God's will that we know him and love him, and that if we cultivate holy awe, we will have deep peace and gentle rest, and everything he does will bring us delight.

So now I have told you about fifteen showings, which God delivered to my consciousness, renewed by illuminations and inspirations from, I hope, the same spirit that revealed them all those years ago. The first showing began early in the morning, around four, and they lasted until around three o'clock the next day, unfolding one after the other in the most elegant order, in deep quietude.

CHAPTER 66

Raving

The next night, God gave me the sixteenth showing. This revelation completed and confirmed the previous fifteen. I will tell you about that later. For now I think it's important to speak about my weakness, misery, and blindness.

Remember when I said at the beginning "all my pain was suddenly taken from me"? During the entire time that the fifteen showings were unfolding, my pain caused me no distress or sorrow. In the end, everything was concealed, and I saw no more. As soon as I sensed that I was going to live longer, the illness came rushing back into me. I felt it first in my head, accompanied by a loud noise, and without warning my body was suddenly overcome by sickness, just as it had been before, and I was so barren and dry it was as if I had never experienced the consolation in the first place. I moaned like a wretch, grieving for the pain I felt in my body and the lack of comfort I could find in my soul.

Then a member of my religious community stopped by to see how I was doing. "I have been raving today," I told him. He laughed loud and heartily. "The cross in front of my face seemed to me to be bleeding profusely," I admitted. When I said this, his

181

expression grew very serious, and he seemed to be awestruck. I was immediately ashamed, amazed by my own recklessness. *This man takes every word I say seriously*, I thought, *even though I told him no more than this one thing.*

When I saw the great respect with which he treated what I said, I felt guilty. I had the urge to confess, but I couldn't possibly explain what I had seen to any priest at that time. *Why should a priest believe me*, I thought, *when I make it sound like nothing more than delirium, as if I did not believe in our Lord God?* But I did believe in him when I saw him, and it was my intention at that time to believe in him forever and never stop. Still, like a fool, I let this clarity pass from my mind.

Look how miserable I was! It felt like a terrible transgression and a grave unkindness to my Beloved to allow a little bit of physical pain, combined with a hearty dose of folly, to make me so carelessly turn away from all the strength and comfort these blessed showings had given me. Here you see what I am like when left to myself. But even though I abandoned him in this way, our gracious God never let me go.

Dream of the Fiend

I lay very still until night fell, trusting in his mercy. And then I began to sleep. As soon as I dozed off, it seemed to me that a fiend was clutching me by the throat and thrusting his face into my face. He looked like a young man, but his bone structure was exceedingly narrow and elongated. I had never seen anything like it. His skin was red, like the color of newly fired roofing tiles, with black specks, like black holes, all over it. But it was much uglier than clay tiles. His hair was rusty red, chopped short in the front, with long sideburns. He snarled at me with a vicious expression, revealing huge, nasty, gleaming teeth. He did not have a regular body, but held me by the throat with his hairy paws. He was trying to kill me, but he couldn't.

Unlike any of my other visions, this horrible apparition came to me in sleep. Throughout the entire experience I entrusted myself to the mercy of God to save and protect me. When our gracious Lord woke me, there was hardly any life left in me. The people who had been sitting with me, watching over me, wet my temples, and my racing heart began to relax.

At that point, a plume of smoke slipped in from under the door. It emitted intense heat and a foul stench. *"Benedicte domine!"* I cried. "Everything is on fire!" I thought there was a physical fire, and that it was going to burn us all to death. "Don't you smell it?" I asked the people around me. "No," they answered. "Blessed be God," I said, relieved that it was just the spirit of evil who had come to tempt me alone.

I immediately took refuge in what our Beloved had revealed to me earlier that same day. I also turned to my faith in Holy Church, for I regarded these as being of equal value, and I fled to them both for comfort. In that moment, everything vanished. I was washed with a deep sense of peace and repose, without a trace of physical illness or spiritual anxiety.

CHAPTER 67

The Kingdom of My Heart

Then our Beloved opened my spiritual eye and showed me my soul in the center of my heart. I saw my soul as vast as if it were a boundless realm, a blessed kingdom, and a prosperous, vibrant city. Our beloved Jesus—truly human, truly Divine—sat in the middle of that place. He was tall and handsome, the most honorable leader, the most awesome ruler, the most exalted master. He was splendidly draped in the finest robes, sitting calmly in dignity and equanimity, guiding and guarding heaven and earth and all that is.

The humanity sits with the Divinity in peace, yet the Divinity alone is in command, without agents or intermediaries, exerting no effort. The soul is completely absorbed by the Godhead, who is perfect Power, perfect Wisdom, and perfect Goodness. Christ will never move from the place he takes in our soul. We are his home of homes, his eternal dwelling. In showing me this, God revealed the utter delight he experiences in creating the human soul. Just as the Father has the power to make a creature, and the Son has the knowledge to make a creature, the Holy Spirit had the desire to create our souls, and so it was done. And so the blessed Trinity endlessly rejoices in the making of the human being, for he saw without beginning what would delight him without end. Everything God has created emanates his mastery.

His True Home

I was given an illustration at that time to help me understand this. I pictured someone being taken to a wonderful kingdom ruled by a great lord. When he beheld the beauty of the landscape below, he was moved to go up to the high place from which the master presided over his realm. After all, he reasoned, the place where the lord dwells must be the most honorable place. In this way I understood that our soul could never find rest in anything that is beneath it. When the soul rises above all created things and enters its true essence, it cannot maintain its focus on itself. Instead, its gaze shifts to God and blissfully fixes on him. God is the Creator who dwells in the center of our own being, which is his true home.

As I see it, the most exalted light and brightly shining radiance in the whole city is the love of God. What could make us rejoice more than to see that God rejoices in us? I realized that if the blessed Trinity could have made the human soul any better, any more beautiful, with any more dignity than it was made, he would not have been wholly satisfied. As it is, he created our soul to be as lovely, as good, and as precious as he could make it, and so he is endlessly pleased with us. He wants our hearts to be lifted above the depths of this world and all the empty sorrows we suffer here and rejoice in God.

CHAPTER 68

You Will Not Be Overcome

It was a delicious sight and a soothing revelation to perceive God's joy in such a way. To be able to contemplate this while we are here on earth is a great help to us and is also pleasing to God. The soul who contemplates God makes itself like the one whom it contemplates. By his grace, such a soul ones itself to him, in peace and rest.

It made me especially happy to see him sitting, for the steadiness of this pose suggests eternal abiding. He confirmed then that he was the One who had shown me everything before. Once I had carefully considered all this and reflected on it over time, our Beloved very humbly and sweetly repeated these words to me, without opening his lips or emitting a sound: "Be well aware that it was not a hallucination you saw today. Accept it, believe it, trust in it, hold it close and allow it to comfort you, and you will not be overcome."

Just as the first words that Christ revealed to me, referring to his blessed passion, were, "With this the spirit of evil is overcome," he uttered these last words with equal truth and faithfulness: "You will not be overcome." This teaching and the comfort it brings are meant for all of us. And he said these words insistently, with great clarity, to reinforce the certainty and strength I would need to face every tribulation that was to come.

He did not say, *you will not be tempted; you will not be troubled; you will not be distressed*. What he said was, "You shall not be overcome." God wants us to pay attention to these words and be strong in absolute trust, in both well and woe. Just as he loves and delights in us, it is his will that we love and delight in him, and fully trust in him, and all will be well.

Soon after this, everything was hidden, and nothing more was revealed to me.

CHAPTER 69

Keep Yourself in the Faith

Then the fiend came again, with all his heat and his stink, and kept me very occupied. The odor was vile and painful, and the physical heat was terribly oppressive. I also heard a garbled chattering, as if two people were talking at the same time. It sounded like they were engaged in a contentious debate about some important matter, muttering in low voices. I could not understand a word they said. This all seemed to be meant to move me to despair. It sounded like people mocking those of us who say our prayers in a lame way, using only the coarse words of our mouth without the devout intention of the heart, neglecting the wise effort we owe to God in prayer.

Our Beloved gave me the grace to powerfully trust in him and to comfort myself by speaking words aloud, as I would to someone else whom I was trying to console. But I found it impossible to reconcile this chaotic internal scene with any experience from my ordinary life. I fixed my physical gaze on that same cross that had comforted me before and occupied my tongue with speaking about Christ's passion and reciting the creed of Holy Church. My heart was clinging to God with all my trust and all my might.

Your task is to keep yourself in the faith, I thought privately, *so that you can avoid being snatched by the Adversary. From now on if you concentrate on avoiding sin that would be an excellent activity for you.* It seemed to me that if I were truly safe from missing the mark, I would be completely protected from the fiends of hell and the enemies inside my own soul.

The spirits of evil occupied me in this way all night long until dawn. Then suddenly they were all gone. They all passed away, and nothing was left but their odor, which lingered for quite a while. I scorned that fiend, and so I was delivered from him by virtue of Christ's passion. It is through this that the spirit of evil is overcome, just as Christ said it would be.

CHAPTER 70

Denying Truth

Throughout this holy showing our Beloved helped me to understand that although the vision would pass, faith perseveres, by his grace and his own goodwill. He did not leave me any sign or token to remember the revelations. But he left me with his own sacred word embedded in my understanding, directing me to believe what I had seen. And so I do. Blessed may he be!

I do think that the One who revealed this truth to me is our Savior, and that what he revealed to me is our faith. And so I believe it, and I rejoice. When he directed me to keep myself in the faith, entrust myself to it, and comfort myself with it, he planted me there, where I remain rooted in love.

On the very same day that he revealed this blessed truth, I denied it the minute the showings had passed, wretch that I am, and openly attributed my vision to delirium. But our beloved Jesus in his mercy would not let the revelation perish, but showed it to my soul all over again, with even greater plenitude and brighter light. He reinforced the vision with these simple, powerful words: "You can be sure that what you saw was not a hallucination." It was if he had said: *Because the vision passed, you let it go and were not able to or did not know how to sustain it. But know it now, that is, now that you are seeing it.*

He said these words not only for that particular occasion, but also to firmly set this truth as the foundation of my faith. "Accept it," he had said. "Believe it, trust in it, hold it close and allow it to comfort you, and you will not be overcome." When he told me to accept it, his intention was to give this truth an unshakable place in our heart. He wants it to dwell with us in faith until the end of our life and beyond, in the fullness of joy. It is his will that we always have faith in his loving promises, because we know his goodness.

Obstacles

Our faith comes up against various inner and outer obstacles, in the form of our own blindness and our spiritual adversaries. And so our precious Lover helps us, giving us all kinds of spiritual insights and teachings of truth, internally and externally, by which we can know him. Whatever way he reveals himself, he wants us to perceive him wisely, receive him sweetly, and keep ourselves faithfully in him. There is no goodness above faith in this life, as I see it, and there is no spiritual health below it. Rather, it is the Beloved's will that we maintain our center there.

Only through his goodness and his own action of grace can we possibly remain strong in our faith. When he permits us to be tested by various spiritual challenges, our faith grows even stronger. If we did not experience any opposition, our faith would not deserve any reward. At least this is what I understood the Lord's meaning to be.

CHAPTER 71

His Three Faces

The blessed face that our Beloved turns toward us is a happy one—joyous and sweet. He sees us lost in love-longing, and he wants to see a smile on our souls, because our delight is his reward. And so I hope that he draws our outer expression inward and makes us all one with him and with each other, in everlasting joy.

I saw three expressions on our Lord's countenance. The first was the face of passion. This is what he showed us while he was here with us in this life, dying. Although it is sad and tragic to behold this face, it is also joyous, for he is Divine. The second is the face of compassion. This is what he shows all his lovers who are in need of empathy and mercy, reassuring us that we will be protected. The third is his true and eternal face, the blessed face he shows us most, the face that will last forever.

In our times of pain and sorrow, he reveals the aspect of his passion on the cross, sharing his own strength to help us bear our suffering. In our times of missing the mark, he reveals the aspect of compassion, which powerfully protects us and helps defend against our adversaries. These two are the expressions he reveals most in this life, mingled with a glimpse of the third—his true blessed face—as we will behold it in the world-to-come.

This is the face of grace and inspiration, which sweetly illumines the life of the spirit, keeping us in true faith, hope, and love. It is a face that inspires devotion and gives rise to contrition. It evokes contemplation and instills every kind of consolation. The blessed face of our Lord accomplishes all this inspiring and enlightening by grace.

CHAPTER 72

Grave Error

At this point I need to tell you about the creatures who have committed grave errors and rather than being condemned for it live in everlasting joy in God. I realized that two opposites could not coexist in one spot. The greatest opposites of all are the highest bliss and the deepest pain. Our highest bliss is to have God in the radiance of everlasting life. It is to see him truly, feel him sweetly, and hold him peacefully in the totality of joy.

In this showing I saw that sin is the fiercest opponent of this bliss. As long as we keep missing the mark, we will not be able to clearly see his blessed face. The more severe and terrible our transgressions are, the farther we fall away (for the time being) from that blessed sight. The sorrow and pain of sin often make us feel as if we were in danger of death, on the threshold of hell. During those times, we are deadened to the true sight of his blessed face.

I saw that we are never dead in the eyes of God nor does he ever leave us. But I also saw that he cannot enjoy his full bliss in us until we enjoy our full bliss in him. We are ordained by nature to behold his beautiful, blessed face and see him truly, and we are brought to this by grace. So I realized that we are holy creatures of endless life and there really is no such thing as mortal sin. We suffer the consequences of grave error for a short time, and then he redeems us.

The more clearly the soul sees his blessed face by the grace of loving, the more it longs to see him in his totality. It is true that our Beloved dwells within us and is here with us, calling to us and enfolding us in his tender love and will never, ever leave us. It is also true that he is closer to us than the heart can think and the tongue can tell. Still, we cannot stop moaning and weeping and yearning for the time when we will be able to look directly into his blessed countenance and see him clearly. No woe can remain in the face of that radiance. There will be no lack of well-being there.

Mirth and Mourning

In this I saw cause for mirth and cause for mourning. It is a matter of mirth that our Beloved, our Creator, lives inside us and that we live in him. This is because of his great goodness and the faithfulness in which he keeps us safe. It is a matter of mourning that our spiritual eye can be so blind and that we become weighed down with the burden of mundane life and the darkness of our own imperfections so that we are no longer able to look our Beloved in the eye or clearly perceive his beautiful, blessed face. No, this darkness prevents us from even daring to believe in his great love and faithful protection.

This is why I say that we cannot stop grieving and weeping. I do not mean that physical tears pour from our eyes. I interpret this weeping more as a spiritual response to the natural desire of the soul to see the face of God. This longing can be so deep and so powerful that if God were to give us all the splendor he ever created in heaven or on earth for our own enjoyment but withheld the sight of his own beautiful face, we still would not be able to stop crying until we truly see the blessed face of our Beloved. And if we were in all the pain the heart can think or the tongue can tell and yet could see his beautiful, blessed face, then none of this pain would bother us. This blessed sight is the end of all pain to the loving soul and the fulfillment of every joy.

There are three kinds of knowing we need to cultivate. The first is to know our beloved God. The second is to know ourselves, which is to know what we are in God, by nature and by grace. The third is to know with humility what we do to ourselves when we miss the mark. This entire showing was revealed to highlight these three forms of knowledge, as I understand it.

CHAPTER 73

Spiritual Sickness

God gave me this whole teaching in three parts. One was a physical vision, another through words formed in my understanding, and the other in the form of spiritual insight. I have described the physical vision as accurately as I am able and have repeated the exact words my Lord spoke to me. And I have done my best to convey the spiritual insight, but I could never fully put it into words. Nevertheless, I am moved to try and say a little more about it, with God's grace.

God showed me that we suffer from two kinds of spiritual sickness: one is impatience (or indolence); the other is despair (or fearful doubt). He revealed that all human beings tend to miss the mark in general, but he emphasized these two transgressions in particular. These are the insidious temptations that trouble us the most, and he wants to set them right. I am speaking about men and women who, out of love for God, try to do his will and avoid sin whenever possible. And yet we are the ones who, through our spiritual blindness and physical laziness, are most inclined to miss the mark in these very ways. And so God wants us to be aware of them so that we are as likely to refuse them as we do the more obvious transgressions.

197

To help us with this, Christ humbly showed me his patience as he endured his cruel passion and also the joy this passion gave him because of love. He used this as a model for how we might more easily and even gladly bear our own suffering, which pleases our Beloved and benefits us. It is our ignorance of love that causes all the trouble. Even though the qualities of the Trinity are of equal value, the soul receives the greatest understanding through love. Yes! God wants us to root everything in the contemplation and enjoyment of love.

Unreasonable Despondency

Yet when it comes to knowledge of love, it is here that we are most blind. Some of us believe that God is All-Power and *able* to do everything. Others believe that God is All-Wisdom and *knows how* to do everything. But the notion that he is All-Love and *wants* to do everything? There we stop. This ignorance is the greatest obstacle for God's lovers, in my opinion. Even after we've learned to reject sin and follow the rules of Holy Church, a certain fear persists, and it continues to hinder us.

Some of us pay too much attention to ourselves and to the transgressions we have committed in the past. Others of us focus too much on our present, everyday imperfections. It is true that we break our vows and neglect to maintain the purity that our Beloved placed in us. We frequently fall into such misery that we can hardly stand to see it. Perceiving all this makes us so sorry and so sad that it seems impossible to find consolation. We may mistake this fear for humility, but it is merely weakness and blindness.

We do not know how to turn away from this fear as we do with the other temptations we more easily recognize. This comes from lack of true judgment. Of all the attributes of the blessed

Trinity, it is God's will that we ground our faith and take most delight in love. Power and Wisdom submit to us when there is Love. For just as God in his graciousness forgives us after a while once we have made amends, he also wants us to forgive ourselves and let go of this unreasonable despondency and these fearful doubts.

CHAPTER 74

Dread

I recognized four kinds of dread. One is fear of attack, which comes upon us suddenly when we feel vulnerable. This can be a good thing because it can have a purifying effect, much in the same way as an illness or some other physical discomfort can purify us, especially when we bear it patiently.

The next one is fear of pain, which can be useful for stirring us and waking us up to the danger of missing the mark. The person who is fast asleep in sin is temporarily unable to receive the gentle touch of the Holy Spirit. He needs the awakening effect of this fear of pain, this dread of physical death and of spiritual peril. It moves us to seek God's comforting mercy. The fear becomes a point of entry. The blessed inspiration of the Holy Spirit opens our closed heart.

The third is fearful doubt, which draws us into despair. God wants to transform it into love by true acknowledgment of love. It is his will that the bitterness of spiritual doubt transmute into the sweetness of natural love by grace. How could our Beloved be pleased when his lovers doubt his Goodness?

The last one is holy awe. This is the only kind of fear that pleases God. It is the gentlest form of dread. The more of it we have, the less of it we feel, because of the sweetness of the love.

Awe

Love and dread are siblings. They are rooted in us by the Goodness of our Creator, and they will never be taken away. Love is in our nature, and we are given the grace to adore God. Dread is in our nature, and we are given the grace to feel awe. God's grandeur and majesty inspire awe. His Goodness evokes love. It is our nature as his servants to revere him in awe, and it is in our nature as his children to adore him for his goodness. Although holy awe cannot be separated from love, still they are two different things. They do not share the same qualities or functions. But you cannot have one without the other. Whoever has love will also have dread, even if he only feels it a little.

All fears other than reverent awe are not real, and the most dangerous ones are those that come disguised as holiness. This is how you can recognize the difference: The kind of dread that drives us into the arms of the Mother, that makes us run away from all that is not good and fall into the breast of the Divine as a child rushes to his mother's embrace—with all the strength of our mind to acknowledge our vulnerability and our deep need, recognizing the everlasting Goodness of God, seeking only him and cleaving to him for our liberation—this is holy awe. It is gentle and merciful, good and true. Any fear other than this is either wrong or else has the wrong mixed up with it.

Here is the remedy: recognize both forms of dread, and choose the right one. The natural fruits we harvest from holy awe in this life, through the grace-giving action of the Holy Spirit, will ripen in the world-to-come when we stand before God. These gifts will be noble and gracious, sweet and delightful. And so we will be intimate with God through love, and we will be equally humble and courteous to God through awe.

What we want is to hold our God in reverent awe and love him with humble trust. When we revere him with intensity and adore him with humility, our trust is never in vain. The more we trust, the more we please and honor the One we trust. If we lack holy awe and humble love (God forbid!), it would be easy to temporarily misdirect our trust. And so we need to ask our Beloved for the gift of grace so that we can have holy awe and humble love, in our heart and in our actions, for his glory and delight.

CHAPTER 75

Three Kinds of Love-Longing

I saw that God can give us everything we need and that there are three things we need most: love, longing, and compassion. When we receive loving compassion in our times of need, we are protected. And love-longing leads us to paradise. God has a powerful thirst to draw all of humanity into himself. That same thirst has already drawn and drunk many holy souls, who now dwell in endless bliss. He is always gathering his living members, drawing and drinking, and yet still he thirsts and yearns.

I saw three kinds of love-longing in God, but they were all for the same aim. We have these yearnings too, and of the same intensity, and for the same goal. The first is to teach us to know him and to love him more and more, which is also a benefit to us. The second is to take us up into his bliss and release us from the pain of this life. The third is to fill us with boundless joy, which is what will happen on the Last Day and will endure forever. What our faith teaches was confirmed then: all pain and sorrow will end when we are liberated. Not only will we participate in the bliss of the holy souls that came before us, but we will also receive a new joy, flowing out from God and into us, and it will make us whole.

Trembling

These are the good things he has ordained for us since before time began. He keeps these good things hidden and treasured inside himself until the ordained time has come, when we will be strong enough to receive them. Then we shall truly see the reason for all the things he has done, and—even more important—all the things he allowed to happen. The bliss and fulfillment will be so high and so deep, and all created beings will be filled with such wonder and amazement, their reverent awe surpassing any they have ever felt before, that the pillars of heaven itself will vibrate and quake.

Yet there will be no pain in this fear and trembling. Rather, this is the proper response to the absolute majesty of the Divine when his creatures behold him. We tremble and quake with the abundance of joy that fills us, marveling at the greatness of God, our Creator, and lost in wonderment in the face of the smallest thing he has created. Such a sight fills all creatures with wondrous humility and quietude.

And so it is God's will that we desire to see him and know him, and that we are aware of what we are beholding. This vision is both in our nature and a gift of grace. It guides us on the right path and keeps us in true life and ones us with God. God is as great as he is good. To the extent that it is right to love him for his goodness, it is right to be in awe of his greatness. Reverent awe is the proper response to the supreme beauty of the Divine. The love and awe we feel for him now will be infinitely expanded when at last we behold his face. Of course all the heavens and the earth will tremble and quake!

CHAPTER 76

Sins of Others

I do not have much more to say about reverent awe than I have already said. I am well aware, however, that the only souls God showed me were the ones in awe of him. I am equally aware that any soul that truly accepts the teachings of the Holy Spirit will reject the ugliness and horribleness of sin more vehemently than all the pains of hell. For the soul that beholds the face of the Divine does not despise hell, but sin itself. And so it is God's will that we become aware of our transgressions and pray earnestly and labor diligently and seek humbly, so that we do not fall blindly back into our old imperfections. And let us pray that if we do fall, we get quickly back up again, for the greatest pain a soul can have is to see that she has turned away from her Beloved.

And when the sins of others come to mind, the soul that wants peace should flee from such thoughts as she would run from the pains of hell. She should seek within God for the remedy to help her resist this impulse to judge, for when we pay attention to the faults of others, a thick mist descends over the eyes of the soul, and for the time being we cannot see the beauty of the Divine. The only exception to this is when we view other people's imperfections with sorrow on their behalf, with sincere compassion for them, and with holy desire for God to be with them. Otherwise, the soul who focuses on these things will be troubled and tempted and hindered.

False Fears

In this showing, I received understanding of two opposites: one is the pinnacle of wisdom any creature can attain in this life; the other is the utmost folly. The wisest thing any creature can do is to act in accordance with the will and guidance of the supreme Friend. This blessed friend is Christ. We need to bind ourselves to his will and guidance, and join ourselves ever more intimately with him, no matter what state we are in. For whether we are clean or unclean, we are always the same in his love. In well or in woe, he wants us to never run away from him.

Because of our inconsistency, we often fall into error. Through the temptations of the Adversary and our own folly and blindness, we miss the mark again and again. This is when a voice in our head whispers, "See? It is obvious to you that you are a fool, a wrongdoer, and also unfaithful. You break your vows all the time. You continually promise your Beloved that you will do better next time, and then you fall right back into the same muck and waste your precious time on nothing of value." (Sloth, as I see it, is the gateway to sin for creatures that have given themselves to serving the Divine in loving contemplation.) These tendencies to miss the mark make us afraid to appear before our gracious God.

But this is the voice of the Adversary. He will try to throw us off track with his false fears about our wretchedness, threatening us with imaginary pain. His intention is to make us so gloomy and weary that we forget the beautiful face of our everlasting Friend.

CHAPTER 77

A Beautiful Humility

Our good God showed me the hatred in the spirit of evil. When I say "the spirit of evil," what I mean is everything that is counter to peace and love. Through our weakness and folly it is inevitable that we stumble, but we are elevated to ever-greater joy through the mercy and grace of the Holy Spirit. If the spirit of evil gains anything from our falling (in which he does take great delight), he loses infinitely more when we get back up in loving-kindness and humility. This glorious rising causes the spirit of evil so much suffering because of the hatred he has for our souls, which burns inside him as a perpetual fire of envy. But all the sorrow he tries to impose on us turns back on himself.

Here is the remedy: we acknowledge our misery and flee into the arms of the Divine. The more swiftly we do this, the more it will benefit us to be near him. And so, with intention, let us say: *I know that I have earned my pain, and that our Beloved is All-Power and can punish me mightily. He is All-Wisdom and knows all the reasons to chastise me. But he is also All-Goodness, and he loves me tenderly.* It is good for us to return again and again to this contemplation.

It is a beautiful humility when, through the mercy and grace of the Holy Spirit, we willingly and cheerfully accept the challenges

and hardships our Lord presents to us. All we have to do is cultivate an attitude of contentment with God and all his works, and
then we will find that his chastening touch is tender and gentle.
He did not show me anything specific about taking on penances.
What he did show me in great detail and in a deeply loving manner was that we need to bear the burdens he gives us with humility and patience, remembering Christ's blessed passion. When we
remember what Christ went through, with love and compassion,
then we share in his suffering, just as the friends who witnessed
it suffered with him.

He says: *Do not accuse yourself so much, telling yourself that
your tribulations and sorrows are all your fault. It is not my will
for you to be unreasonably depressed or despondent. For I tell
you that no matter what you do, you will have woe. And so it
is my will that you recognize what you are always and already
going through as your penance, and that you humbly accept it
as such. Then you will truly see that the whole of your life is an
opportunity for atonement, which is very beneficial to you.*

Be Like Christ

This earth is a prison, this life is a penance, and he wants us to
rejoice in the remedy. The remedy is that our Beloved is with us,
keeping us safe and guiding us into the fullness of joy. The One
who will be our bliss when we are there is our protector when
we are here. True love and unshakable trust open our way to
paradise.

Let us rush into the arms of the Divine, where we shall be
comforted. Let us touch him, and we shall be purified. Let us
cleave to him, and we shall be safe and secure from every kind of
danger. Our gracious God wants us to be as friendly with him as
the heart can think or the soul can desire. Yet let us not so care-

lessly accept this familiarity that we forsake courtesy. For our Lord is as courteous as he is friendly. He is both supreme friendliness and the very essence of courtesy.

Christ wishes for all the creatures that will be with him forever in paradise to be as much like him as possible here on earth. To be as perfectly like Christ as we can in all things is to have true salvation and complete happiness. If we do not know how to do this, let us ask him to teach us. This would be to his great honor and true delight. Blessed may he be!

CHAPTER 78

Adjusting Our View

Our Beloved in his mercy does not show us our faults except by the light of his own self, which transmutes the horror. It is his will that we have knowledge of four things. First, he is our ground. It is from him that we have our life and being. Next, when we are sinning, he protects us powerfully and mercifully against our ferocious adversaries who would like nothing more than to see us fail. (We have no idea of the peril we are in and how badly we need God's help. This ignorance gives the spirit of evil ample opportunity to assail us.) Third, he graciously guards us and lets us know when we get off track. Finally, he steadfastly waits for us and does not change his position, for he wants us to be transformed and one-ed to him in love, as he is already united to us.

And so, through the grace-filled knowledge he gives us, we can perceive our transgressions without despair and gain benefit. For seeing these things truly humbles us and breaks down our pride and presumption. It's important for us to recognize that of ourselves we are nothing. And so by glimpsing the little he reveals to us, the bulk of what remains becomes diluted and dissipates. The full view of our imperfections would be too painful to take in, and so, in his courtesy, he adjusts it for us.

Through contrition and grace, this humble knowledge breaks us down from everything that is not of God. Then our blessed Beloved heals us and joins us to himself. This breaking and healing and melding are available to all of humanity. For he who is highest and closest to God can see himself as imperfect and needy right along with me. I who am the lowest of those who will be liberated can take equal comfort with the ones who are highest. Our Beloved has united us all in his love.

Pause

At the time when he revealed to me that I was bound to sin, I was so taken up in the joy of beholding him that I did not really attend to the revelation. And so our courteous Lord paused and would not show me more until he gave me the grace and the will to pay attention. In this way he taught me that even if we are lifted to the heights of contemplation by the special gift of our Beloved, we need to have knowledge of our weaknesses and errors, too. Without this awareness we cannot have true humility, and without humility we cannot be liberated. I also saw that we cannot acquire this knowledge on our own, or from our spiritual adversaries, who do not wish us much good but rather, if they had their way, would prefer to see us never attain our goal until the end of time.

And so we owe everything to God, who, out of love, shows us all we need to know about ourselves.

CHAPTER 79

Whole of Humanity

There was more to this revelation about how I would continue to miss the mark. At first, I applied this teaching to my individual self, because at the time I was not moved to see it otherwise. But the great and gracious comfort that followed made me realize that he meant this insight for the whole of humanity. All of us who miss the mark—and I am one of them—will be enfolded by the vast generosity and consolation of the Divine. Here I was reminded too that I must not focus on the imperfections of others but instead take responsibility for my own. The only exception to this would be if my reflections could be helpful and comforting to my fellow spiritual seekers.

The other thing I learned from this showing was to be careful about becoming overly anxious about my own transgressions. I cannot know how I might fall, and I am not capable of judging the severity of my own errors when I do. I very much wanted certain knowledge of these things, but it was not given to me. At the same time our courteous Beloved showed me the limitless and unchangeable certainty of his love. He reassured me that, by his great goodness and inwardly protective grace, his love for us and our love for him would never, ever be separated. And so my awe keeps me humble, which saves me from presumption, and the blessed revelation of love fills me with comfort and joy, which saves me from despair.

Love Lesson

This entire friendly showing of our gracious Beloved was a love-lesson. It was a lovely, gracious teaching offered from his own being to console our souls. He wants us to know by the sweetness of his familiar love that everything we see or feel, both inwardly and outwardly, that is in opposition to this love, is not of God. For instance, if we allow our knowledge of his abundant love to make us careless about the way we live or the condition in which we keep our hearts, then we need to beware. This inclination, if it arises, is not rooted in truth, and we need to dig it out and discard it, for it has nothing to do with the divine will.

When our frailty and blindness cause us to stumble and fall, then our gracious God touches us, stirs us, and calls us. He wants us to squarely see our wretchedness and humbly acknowledge our error. But he does not want us to get stuck there, so vigilant and self-accusing that we feel completely miserable about ourselves. He wants us to quickly shift our attention to him, for he stands alone, constantly waiting for us. He is sorrowing and grieving, longing for us to return to him, eager to take us into himself. We are his joy and his delight. He is our remedy and our life.

CHAPTER 80

ABCs

Humanity is grounded by three things in this life, and by these three things God is honored and we are protected, assisted, and liberated. The first is the use of humanity's natural reason. The second is the common teaching of Holy Church. The third is the inward, grace-giving action of the Holy Spirit. God is the foundation of our natural reason. God is the teaching of Holy Church. And God is the Holy Spirit.

These are three different gifts that he wants us to cherish and pay attention to. They are each important, and they are constantly working together in us. He wants us to see them as being as basic as our ABCs. That is, we will gain elementary understanding of certain things in this life that will be fully revealed in the world-to-come.

And So He Waits

Our faith teaches us that God-as-Christ took our human nature, and that Christ performed all the great acts that resulted in our salvation, and that he continues to act now in this final age. He dwells here with us, guiding us and taking care of us, and he brings us divine bliss. He will do this as long as any soul remains on earth to be brought into paradise. If there were even one soul left, he would be with that one all alone until he had brought it up into his bliss.

I believe in angels, as the priests have taught us, but I did not see anything about their ministrations in my showings. God himself is nearest and humblest, highest and lowest, and he does everything. God gives our souls what they need in this life and fulfills our deepest desires in the world-to-come.

When I say that our Beloved is sorrowing and grieving, that means that all our truest feelings of contrition and compassion— all our longing for oneing with God—are actually Christ within us. Even though most of us rarely sense his yearning, it is always with him until we are all delivered from our woe. Love never allows him to let go of his compassion. Whenever we miss the mark and stop remembering him and guarding our own souls, then Christ steps in and takes responsibility for us.

And so he waits, sorrowing and grieving. Therefore, out of reverence and kindness, we should turn ourselves quickly over to him and never leave him alone. He is alone here with each of us, always. That is to say, it is for our sake alone that he is here. Whenever I am alienated from him by despair or sloth, I make a place for my Beloved to stand alone inside me. This is true for all of us. Even if we frequently miss the mark, his goodness never permits us to be alone. He is always with us. He tenderly dismisses our transgressions and always shields us from blame in his sight.

CHAPTER 81

His Resting Place

There were many ways our beloved God manifested himself to this creature—both in heaven and on earth—but I saw that the only place he rested was in the human soul. He showed himself on earth in the sweet incarnation and in his blessed passion. He also revealed himself in the form of a pilgrimage; that is, he is leading us through this life on earth toward his bliss in heaven. He has chosen the soul of humanity as his resting place, and this is the great city and honorable throne from which he lovingly reigns. He will never rise or move away from this spot inside us. What a wondrous and magnificent place it is where the Beloved dwells!

God wants us to pay attention to his gracious touch, rejoicing in his unconditional love rather than sorrowing in our own failings. For of all the things we could do it is our surrender to live with our burdens in joy and gratitude that brings him the most glory. His love for us is so tender that he sees all we go through in this life as a special kind of martyrdom that purifies and makes us ready for oneing with him. The greatest penance of all is our natural longing for him. He himself creates this yearning in us, and he helps us to bear it.

His loves makes him long for us. His wisdom, truth, and righteousness make him forgive us. This is how he would like for us to see it. This life is our natural penance and highest task. Our trials will continue until the time when he makes us whole and gives us himself as our reward. And so he wants us to set our hearts on our transition, that is, from the pain we feel to the joy we trust.

CHAPTER 82

Mistakes Are Inevitable

When our good God revealed the sorrowing and grieving of the soul, this is what he meant:

"I am well aware that you live for my love, joyfully bearing the burdens that come to you. And yet it makes you sad that you cannot seem to avoid missing the mark in this life. Even if you could live entirely free from error, I know that you would still suffer all that woe for the sake of my love, cheerfully surrendering to every kind of tribulation and distress that could befall you. But please do not let the mistakes you did not mean to make bother you."

What I understood from this is that the Master sees the servant with compassion and not with blame. This passing life does not require that we live without sin. He loves us endlessly, and we miss the mark constantly. He points out our transgressions gently, and we lament prudently. We turn ourselves over to contemplation of his mercy, cleaving to his love and goodness, recognizing that he is our remedy, aware that it is inevitable that we will make mistakes. By seeing our imperfections we gain humility, reinforcing our faith in his everlasting love.

Our gratitude and praise in the face of our predicament bring him great joy. God's will that we live in longing and rejoicing is so powerful, it made me realize that anything opposed to this cannot possibly come from him, but rather from the spirit of evil. He wants us to know this by the sweet gracious light of his love.

Rising or Falling

If there is a single soul on this earth who never misses the mark, I am not aware of it, because it was not shown to me. But this was shown: That whether rising or falling, we are always graciously enfolded in one love. In the sight of God we do not fall, and in our own sight we do not stand. While both of these perspectives are true, as I see it, the way God sees is the highest truth. God's will for us to know the higher truth binds us ever more closely to him. What is most helpful, I realized, is for us to hold both truths together in this life. The higher perspective gives us spiritual solace and true joy, while the other keeps us humble. But our beloved God wants us to focus more from the higher point of view until we are brought up to our full and endless joy, where we shall receive him as our reward.

CHAPTER 83

Life, Love, Light

I received inspiration, vision, and feeling regarding three attributes of God. The strength and outcome of the whole revelation rest on these. They are: life, love, and light. There is a wondrous familiarity in life, a gentle courtesy in love, and an everlasting kindness in light. I saw these three properties as a single Goodness, and I wished with all my might for my consciousness to be joined to that Goodness. I pondered with awe that our mind resides in God, and I understood that our ability to think is a gift from God, one that is built into our human nature. This realization filled me with wonder and a sense of sweet harmony.

Our faith is a light that naturally flows from our Father God, our Mother Christ, and our good Lord, the Holy Spirit. They lead us through this passing life and into our endless day. This light is carefully measured out and available to us when we need it in the depths of the night. This light is the source of our life, and the night is the cause of our pain and woe. We earn boundless gratitude from God for our suffering, because we willingly acknowledge and believe in our light, and we walk wisely and powerfully in it.

When our suffering ends, at last our eyes will open, and in that sudden clarity our light will be total. This light is God, our Father-Mother, our Creator, and the Holy Spirit, inside Christ Jesus, our Liberator. I saw that our faith is our light in the darkness of night, and that light is God, our endless day.

CHAPTER 84

Endless Day

This light is love, which the Wisdom of God generously measures out for us. The light is not bright enough for us to clearly perceive our endless day, nor is it completely hidden from us. It is just enough for us to live righteously, offering ourselves in service to the glory of God and earning his boundless gratitude.

So love keeps us in faith and hope. Faith and hope lead us to love. And all shall be love in the end.

I had three kinds of understanding about this light of love: one is uncreated love; the next is love in creation; and the third is love that is shared. Uncreated love is God. Love in creation is our soul in God. The love that is shared is virtue, which is the gift of love in action. We love God for herself, and we love ourselves in God, and we love all that God loves for her sake.

CHAPTER 85

It Is So

I marveled at this vision, for in spite of our blindness here on earth and the foolish ways we live our lives, our endlessly gracious God still holds us in the highest regard and rejoices in all we do and are. We please her most by wisely and truly believing in her love, and rejoicing with her and in her. Just as we shall one day come to live in the endless bliss of God, praising her and thanking her with all our hearts, so she has loved us and known us in her boundless foresight since before time began. She created us inside this love-without-beginning, and she protects us within that same love. She will never allow anything to impede our ultimate joy.

And so when the final judgment comes and we are all brought up to the heavenly realms, we shall clearly see in God all the secrets that are hidden from us now. Then none of us will be moved in any way to say, *Lord, if only things had been different, all would have been well.* Instead, we shall all proclaim in one voice, *Beloved One, may you be blessed, because it is so: all is well. We see now that everything happened in accordance with your divine will, ordained before the beginning of time.*

CHAPTER 86

Love Was His Meaning

This book began by the grace of a gift from God, but its work, as I see it, is not yet done. For the sake of love, let us all pray together, uniting our efforts with the divine will. Our Beloved wants us to pray by giving thanks and trusting and rejoicing in him. This is what he meant when he so cheerfully said, "I am the ground of your prayer."

I clearly saw that our Beloved gave these showings so that we would understand love better. Through this understanding he gives us the grace to love him and cleave to him. We are his divine treasure, and he holds us in such profound love here on earth that he will give us more light, solace, and joy in the world-to-come, drawing our hearts from the sorrow and darkness in which we are now living.

Throughout the time of my showings, I wished to know what our Beloved meant. More than fifteen years later, the answer came in a spiritual vision. This is what I heard. "Would you like to know our Lord's meaning in all this? Know it well: love was his meaning. Who revealed this to you? Love. What did he reveal to you? Love. Why did he reveal it to you? For love. Stay with this and you will know more of the same. You will never know anything but love, without end."

And so what I saw most clearly was that love is his meaning. God wants us to know that he loved us before he even made us, and this love has never diminished and never will. All his actions unfold from this love, and through this love he makes everything that happens of value to us, and in this love we find everlasting life. Our creation has a starting point, but the love in which he made us has no beginning, and this love is our true source.

Thanks be to God!

About the Author

Mirabai Starr is an award-winning author of creative nonfiction and contemporary translations of sacred literature. She taught philosophy and world religions at the University of New Mexico-Taos for twenty years and now teaches and speaks internationally on contemplative practice and inter-spiritual dialog. A certified bereavement counselor, Mirabai helps mourners harness the transformational power of loss. Her latest book, *Wild Mercy: Living the Fierce and Tender Wisdom of the Women Mystics,* was named one of the "Best Books of 2019." She lives with her extended family in the mountains of northern New Mexico.

Hampton Roads Publishing Company
... for the evolving human spirit

Hampton Roads Publishing Company
publishes books on a variety of subjects,
including spirituality, health,
and other related topics.

For a copy of our latest trade catalog, call (978) 465-0504
or visit our distributor's website at *www.redwheelweiser.com.*
You can also sign up for our newsletter and special offers by
going to *www.redwheelweiser.com/newsletter.*